ADVANCE PRAISE FOR BOUNCE BACK

Rich has put together a very comprehensive and useful guide to navigate through these unprecedented times. The challenges can be overwhelming, particularly when your personal livelihood and possibly your life savings are on the line. This level-headed and thorough approach, backed by years of Rich's experience, can help pave the road for a way out of business difficulties and set the foundation for a sustainable prosperous business.

Chris Vasiloff
Retired Senior Vice President of
Ingersoll-Rand Company and current
small business investor and entrepreneur

Richard, with his vast experience and sound advice, has for years helped businesses not only succeed, but thrive. Rich's newest release, *Bounce Back: Survive and Thrive in a Business Crisis*, condenses that knowledge into very easily understood and applied processes. This book will help any business owners to manage through constantly changing markets, reevaluate their strategies, and redirect their efforts to achieve the highest possible rewards.

Dan Brownlee
CEO, Brownlee Lumber, Inc.

BOUNCE BACK

Survive and Thrive in a Business Crisis

Richard Mowrey

Find additional resources at:
www.RichMowrey.com

Copyright © 2020 Richard D. Mowrey

Published by Groundhog New Media

Edited by Nina Shoroplova

Layout Design by Amit Dey

ISBN: 978-0-9978801-6-8

TABLE OF CONTENTS

INTRODUCTION

When you are in the middle of a business crisis, it takes some courage to acknowledge the extent of the problems. Not to mention finding the energy and focus to work your way out. This book, *Bounce Back*, provides some proven historic wisdom and techniques that will help you survive a business interruption. Please take the time required to absorb the knowledge gathered and presented herein. This information was taught to me ... and taught by me. It was assembled and distilled over decades of business consulting. By applying this know-how you should be able to help your business bounce back with much less stress. And then, thrive in a changed environment!

When your business has internal problems, it is a little easier to create a revival plan. It is a lot more difficult when the entire economy is in distress. Quite often businesses experience disruptions from one of the dismal D's (Disability, Divorce, Death, or Business Disruption.) All but the latter are associated with problems of the owner.

Business troubles can come from internal actions or lack of action. It is more likely for a business's deep distress to arrive as part of a general economic downturn. The fact that other businesses are struggling makes it harder to regain lost ground and to return to profitability.

The problem addressed here is predicated on finding the right set of responses and actions to survive and thrive in a broad crisis. That is not to say that the principles and processes cannot be successfully applied to a less-demanding situation. When the problems are more internal, there are some advantages you will not have when the entire economy declines. In theory, developing a recovery plan is easier if the marketplace still has significant strength.

When all around you are in distress, it takes a larger measure of strategic and innovative thinking to find a way to survive. And ... finding the right combination of strategies and actions to thrive becomes more problematic. This is due, in large part, to the higher level of uncertainty about the future. When your customers' customers are not honoring their invoices, their problems can quickly become your problem. This sobering reality requires a survival-first mindset to get the best results. The different general topics in this book are designed to give you the confidence that you can manage your way forward.

It may take a minor or major makeover of your business to ultimately thrive in a rapidly changing market. That may sound like a major task. It is not nearly as hard to do as it could be to persist with an outdated business model. We will take a look at a historic business failure that is often mentioned in discussions of this nature. This look back and other materials in this book may not be new to you. That does not mean these lessons are any less important to grasp. This information is here to help you create the series of plans and projects required to survive. Once you break out of the economic wilderness, you can establish a new foundation for success. That stride forward will help you create a new platform, one on which you can build a thriving enterprise.

The chapters are grouped to provide you with the option to look ahead or to look back. This structure should accentuate use of your own personal experience in this process. It will also help you to utilize your company's strengths more quickly. Within the text are lists of questions and other action-oriented discussions. These offerings are designed to help you accelerate your response to the crisis. There are also tools and templates provided herein to support your efforts. Their use along with other reference materials will shorten the timeline needed to outline the "next step" actions you must take. They will help you develop and execute your survive and thrive plans.

In a crisis, you do not have the time or the money to schedule an offsite strategic planning session. You simply must plan and act in the short term to position your business for the longer term. The information, tools, and techniques presented here are designed to match this imperative. To meet this challenge, use the twelve-twelve process. Plan the next twelve months of business change and improvement in the next twelve days! That is a two-week planning period. (Take a day off each week to clear your mind and renew your energy.)

Ideally, you should read through the entire book and then go back and begin the specific work. Each topic area is laid out to prompt actions to help with the survival of your business. This approach will afford you the benefit of broader strategic thinking and should help prompt the integration of creative, insightful, uplifting strategies. Identification of the right strategies and actions should carry you and your business to new heights on the other side of an economic crisis.

Do not despair when you realize that this is a difficult process. It will provide you with an opportunity to really assess where your business is in a changing environment. That knowledge can be golden! Once you have that analysis underway, you are ready to create both your "survive plans" and your "change plans"! You can plan a small or a large operating strategy shift in the next dozen days, a change that will help you develop a much more profitable business a year from now. Now is the time to plan twelve months of effective transformative steps for your business. You can do that in the next twelve days so your business can survive and thrive whatever business crisis you are experiencing.

SURVIVE and THRIVE

in a BUSINESS CRISIS

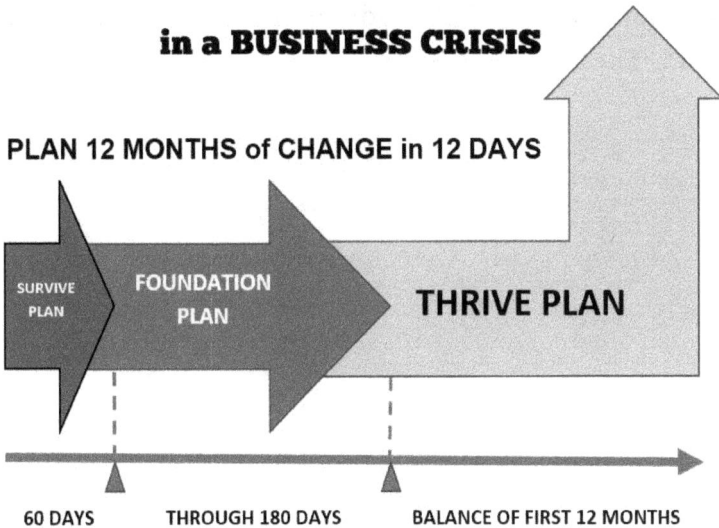

PLAN 12 MONTHS of CHANGE in 12 DAYS

SURVIVE PLAN

FOUNDATION PLAN

THRIVE PLAN

| 60 DAYS | THROUGH 180 DAYS | BALANCE OF FIRST 12 MONTHS |

Here is one of the best quotes to ponder in times of trouble. It has been attributed to Chuck Noll, legendary Pittsburgh Steelers football coach.

"When things are good, they are not as good as you think they are!"

When things are bad, they are not as bad as you think they are!"

Just think of how quickly things have or can change negatively. Things may have been good, but something unexpected smashed that bright picture. This can happen in reverse. It may not take monumental actions to get on a positive track. It should only take acquiring some new knowledge, good thinking, and consistent actions to successfully address the evolving situation at hand. These are all things you can do!

PART 1

SURVIVING WITH THOUGHT, HELP, AND ACTION

What looks like "cracks" in the economy may be the openings to massive future opportunities!

CHAPTER 1

COMMIT TO FINDING A WAY TO SURVIVE

Understanding what is really happening to your company in a developing crisis is no easy task. It is vastly different than prudently planning for the next general economic downward cycle. To survive, you must commit to developing the plans and near-term performance necessary to be in business one more day! Start by finding and applying the power of your business. Once you know what you want to do and what you can do, it is much easier to know what to avoid.

Careful reviewing of the following three principles can help you and your business weather the storms in an economic crisis. This is true whether the problems are broad-based or more unique to your business. To survive in a highly disruptive period, you will have to do things you have never done before. All of which will be difficult ... and necessary! Here are the three most important operating survival principles to take to heart.

1. *Never Run Out of Cash*

It is axiomatic that you should never run out of cash in your business. However, what is critical is to understand exactly what happens to most businesses in a deep drop in economic activity. There certainly are differences between retail, distribution, manufacturing, and service businesses. In practice, however, the problems are the same. The cash flow needs and cycles do vary in these diverse business models. Each one may require a degree of renewed understanding in a crisis.

> **When you are in the middle of a crisis**
> **caused by a disruption in your business,**
> **it is easy to say after the fact, that you**
> **should have planned ahead.**

Yes, you should have sufficient reserves to handle most expected declines in business volume. And ... yes ... you should have arranged the largest possible line-of-credit (LOC) with your financial institution in advanced. You can use a LOC as needed to handle growth in good times and to sustain the business in bad times. But you cannot go back to put those reserves and plans in place now. It is too late after you are plunged into a deep business hole with the corresponding huge drop in revenue.

Once in the wilderness with no clear vision ahead, where there is little if any cash in-flow, the first step is to stop all cash outflows. No payments should be made until you can prioritize exactly what should be paid and when. Concurrent with the stopping of all payments, you should be communicating with the key players in your operation. Here are some ideas and an approach that, once adopted, can make a measurable difference:

Take care of your employees first.

Set aside the cash needed to pay the currently due payroll and associated taxes. Then project the level of staffing needed in the very short-term. Develop your initial survive and thrive plans. Once those rough amounts are known, reserve the existing cash for specific purposes for at least thirty days.

Furlough employees who cannot be directly productive with customer services and production. If at all possible, maintain all employee benefits. Advise them that you are making new plans that you will share with them as soon as they are completed and proven viable.

Make an extra effort to be aware of any special government programs that might help your employees. Sometimes when things are bad, the government develops meaningful support for small businesses. Your bank, accountant, and attorney should be of some assistance in navigating this option. Do not use any such programs until you understand all their contingencies and their related regulatory applications.

Communicate with your major vendors.

Contact all of your critical vendors. Ask for new dating on all outstanding invoices. Negotiate some partial payments as needed to get this courtesy. Be firm and convincing that you just need some time to respond to the newly presented problems. Once you accomplish this, ask for dating on any new purchases in the next sixty days. Most vendors will squawk! But, if you have been faithfully paying them for years, they should allow some new deliveries to occur. They know how important it is to support you so you can resume more normal operations.

Make a tentative plan, to the extent that is possible, to pay all the smaller local vendors' invoices in a timely manner.

These companies may be in exactly the same place you are. They all have families and employees who may be your current or future customers. Act on this portion of your payables as soon as you have your cash flow plan completed. Be sure that these allocated funds are not required for payroll or to keep a reluctant major vendor in the supplier mix.

Prioritize utilities, insurance, and similar critical invoices.

When developing a cash allocation plan for your total package of payables, be sure to recognize utilities and insurances as high priorities. You must keep the lights on and your risks covered to survive.

Talk personally with all of your landlords.

Landlords will be very hesitant to permit you to delay your rent payment. Ask with some solid feeling about the importance of this deferral to your recovery plan. Advise the lessors that you will catch up on the rent payments at a certain time in the not-too-distant future. Twelve months will probably be as long as you can reasonably defer one or two months' rent payments. Ask for what you need for survival. Communicate the reasons for the request and the plans you are developing to transition from a survival mode.

Call your banker and ask for loan-payment deferrals.

You may need a ninety-day period with no mortgage or other loan payments. Again, ask for the flexibility you think you need to be able to allocate your limited cash to other uses. Detail out for them the limited cash flow to the priority payments you are establishing. To the extent that government action in desperate times are set up to backstop the banks, ask about these options. Follow your banker's lead in this area. You may be pleasantly surprised at how helpful a good long-time personal banker can be to you and your business situation. They really do want you to survive and thrive!

For a business that sells on thirty-day terms, as the economy turns down and sales drop, accounts receivable are collected from prior periods. This anomaly can cause many people to feel they are in a much better cash position than they really are. Be aware of this fact and conserve cash.

As the economy and your revenues recover, Accounts Receivable and Work-in-Process will also increase. These normal and other current asset changes are going to have a dramatic increase as your business improves at the sales line. Be prepared! Plan for this cash utilization to occur.

What is often difficult to understand is just how much cash is consumed by working capital in a growth cycle. In normal times, growth in excess of 15% per annum will put a strain on most businesses. In a recovery cycle, percentage growth can be buried by what appears to be smaller absolute growth in working capital requirements. It is these incremental changes that happen faster than normal and put a lot of pressure on the business. They can put a business owner in exactly the place they do not want to be.

To avoid this situation, every business owner should first understand the "cash conversion cycle" in their business. With precise knowledge of the cash conversion cycle, and some basic estimating skills, it is easy to predict the amount of working capital required for a "normal" growth cycle. What is less clear is how much difference there will be in the historic customers' payment processing as they too rebound.

Sales improvements will end when the cash required to support that growth is not available. Without this knowledge in hand and without the support of financial institutions, a business can get into a debilitating cash position at the wrong time.

So, plan for the growth you want and understand the cash you need to support that growth. Ask your banker and vendors for the flexibility required to regain your previous revenue operating levels. Otherwise, you may find yourself running out of cash, which is something you always must avoid.

You should have some expectation that the pressure banks are under will change on the upside of any downturn. Consequently, borrowing will eventually become more difficult. Expect to see more of the lending problems business customers may have experienced in the past.

In summary on this point, know how much cash you will require to survive and reinvent your business and then ask for what you need! Do not be shy! Ask with sensory acuity. Ask with a confident smile. Keep asking until you make the required combination of arrangements to "not run out of cash"!

2. Never Operate without a Written Business Plan

It is surprising how many business owners expect to operate their businesses without written business plans.

Hopefully, you are not in that group. But, if you are, that can now be in the past. Businesses without effective plans will never know how much greater results they would have had if they had taken the time to do some additional thinking and planning. A well-thought-out plan is a required document to know where you want to go and how to get there. That is really the essence of business planning: determining what the businesses will look like at a certain point in the future and what must be done to achieve that end.

When you see your business declining, it is hard to engage in a formal planning process. It is not the formality that makes the planning process valuable. It is the work behind the plan. That is the journey that is needed to initiate a rebound when you find yourself in a deeply depressed business environment.

Each step of the way should be planned to make sure that the results are achieved. You will need to specify short-term survival objectives and long-term strategy implementations to survive and thrive. All major objectives can best be realized by developing a detailed set of projects with clear responsibility and scheduled target dates identified. (Projects may be independent or combine both short-term survival objectives ... and long-term thrive goals.) One of the many things that is critical to success with business planning and operations is to have a measurement system in place or at least in development to assure progress is actually being made.

We will address some of the diagnostic steps; the judicious changes in thinking required; and the planning techniques you can use to develop your shorter-term plans in the balance of this book. In addition, the associated cash flow schedules and inputs to help you figure out how to best address a changing market will be discussed.

Measured systems have proven over time to outperform unmeasured systems by approximately 20%.

The key to success for the business owner is to determine what things should be done and how to measure the actions to accelerate movement along the path. Without doing the work required to effectively develop and implement a business plan, most businesses will underperform. And in difficult economic periods, they could unexpectedly be at significantly increased risk. So, to survive and thrive you need a series of measurable outcomes.

As soon as you lay a foundation for planning, take the following three steps as you read and review the balance of this book:

First, **develop a survival plan** with projected cash flows. Set up a specific cash weekly outflow for each of the first four to eight weeks. Set an ending cash balance objective for week four. Figure out how to operate to end the period with that amount of cash in hand. The key sections to this planning document are the sources and uses of funds and staffing strategies for this short four to eight-week time frame.

Second, prepare a six-month business plan based on all the required changes needed to use your company's strengths to take advantage of the disruption in the marketplace. This is a foundation-building phase. A major objective in this interval, after the survival period, is to establish and lower the "cash flow" break-even point for your business. If you have never determined your business's breakeven operating level this exercise should yield some new insights. This new information can help drive necessary reductions of costs through operating modifications.

A review of the template provided here, with model figures, should help you understand the operation of the analysis. The first step is to determine the breakeven point for your business without any changes.

To do this analysis, study your different operating expenses to see what portion is "fixed." Separate those expenses from the variable expenses in each category, as shown in the template above.

Be sure to recognize that depreciation is a "non-cash" expense and conversely that capital investments (CAP-X) are cash uses not shown on the income statement. Work up the "pre-tax" cash required to make your

[All Dollars in (000)]	Prior Year 20XX	FIXED PORTION	VARIABLE PORTION	Percent of Revenue	BreakEven
Sales Revenue	12,000		12,000	100%	9,750
Total Cost of Goods Sold	8,000	2,000	6,000	50%	6,875
Gross Margin	4,000	-2,000	6,000	50%	2,875
Operating Expenses					
Selling Expense	1,500	300	1,200	10%	1,275
General & Admin. Expenses	1,200	1,200	0	0%	1,200
Total Operating Expense	2,700	1,500	1,200	10%	2,475
Operating EBITDA	1,300	-3,500	4,800	40%	400
Depreciation & Amortizataion	400	0	400	3%	400
Operating Income/(Loss)- EBIT	900	-3,500	4,400	37%	0
Other (Income)/Expenses					
Interest Expense	120	120	0	0%	120
Other (Income)/ Expenses	0		0	0%	
	120	120	0	0%	120
Pre-Tax Income	780	-3,620	4,400	37%	-120
Less: Income Tax @ 30%	234	0	0		0
Net Income /(Loss)	546	-3,620	4,400		-120
Plus: Non-cash Expense	400				400
Less: Working Capital Changes	0				0
Less: -X Investments	0				0
Less: Debt - Principal Payments	280	280			280
SIMPLE CASH FLOW	666	-3,900			0

debt principal payments and compute the total "fixed payments" exhibited in your business. (Your accounting staff or another outside professional can help you do this analysis to keep all the moving parts in proper order. They can do this work in a relatively short time if asked.)

Compute the percentage relationship to revenue for the variable expenses in your system. Observe the variable percentage relationship of the EBITDA (Earnings before interest, depreciation, and amortization) to total revenue. (In the example, this is forty percent (40%). Divide the total "fixed expenses" ($3.9M in the example) by the EBITDA percent to compute the company's break-even revenue level with the current "fixed expenses" in place before adjustment.

Once that is accomplished, the next step is to aggressively review every "fixed" expense to see what portion is partly discretionary and should be reduced. The second step in this restructuring effort is to reduce those expenses and reassess the lowered break-even point. If this new level still exceeds the anticipated revenue and gross margin projection, more work is indicated, both to gain revenue to bounce faster and to change the operation to further reduce the break-even point.

To emphasize this major action, let us look at the situation for this example company. If the projected revenue for the next six months is going to be at a lower annual revenue equivalent of only eight million dollars ($8M), more action is required. This projection should, in turn, prompt the owner to figure out how to reduce the "fixed expenses" down to three million two hundred thousand dollars ($3.2M). This is how the analysis affords the business owner the information required to re-plan operations.

Achieving a "cash flow break-even" position will buy you time and give you some peace of mind as you work toward the larger "bounce back" for your business.

Exercising your thinking on the financial side of this picture should help you as you work "on your business" to change it to meet new market challenges. **Third**, once you have a foundation plan in place, **adopt a strategy to thrive over the next two to three years**. This starts by preparing a strategic plan and a one-year business plan that fully exercises this identified strategy to foster growth in a fast-changing marketplace. (Suggestions on how to do this strategic planning in a shorter-than-traditional period will be presented later in this book.)

3. Never Give Up

Too many business owners look at mounting problems and get stalled in what is the worst possible mental place. There is almost always a path forward if you have the right mindset, the right people to help you, and something of value for your customers. It takes an oversized measure of determination and perseverance to keep moving. Search for the critical inputs to a workable plan and put your thinking cap on. Once plans are in place, it is action and the maintenance of a positive attitude that will make the final difference. Don't let fear and concerns about the unknown control your actions. Ask for the help you need. Plan effectively. Feel the fear and do it anyway ... as the commercial says.

Buy time with prudent, creative actions ... think and rethink before you act. But act in the time frame necessary to resolve the problems in front of you so you can get to the ones you cannot yet see!

The great basketball coach, John Wooden, insisted that his players understand and apply the following principle. It applies to both basketball and management decision-making. You will find that this approach is never more important than at times of crisis and mounting troubles.

Be quick ... but don't hurry!

CHAPTER 2

FUTURE FINANCIAL PERFORMANCE

I t is management's job to be able to assess the operating environment for today and tomorrow and to adjust to the changes as they occur. Disruptions will occur and reoccur. Ideally, managers should pick up early on the trends and reposition the company **before** there are any lasting detrimental impacts from these "outside" forces.

All of the FACTORS in the following areas of the business have a notable effect on financial results. All of your plans, even in a crisis, should take these factors into account. Let's take a quick look at the full list, so you can better understand that statement and, in some manner, rank the level of input priority each group of factors should have ... first in survival plans and then in longer-term thrive plans.

Macro-Economic Factors

General business cycle—assess how long it may be to reach a full recovery.

International economic factors—understand what may hit your plans.

Government policies—include the positive and negative actions anticipated.

Long-term trends—plans should be structured to thrive over time.

Industry Factors

Structure of the marketplace—fully appreciate what has and will change.

Level of competition—constantly survey and gauge your competitors' respective strengths.

Capital intensiveness—know early what new equipment will be required.

Long-term trends—integrate these effected trends into your thrive plans.

Business Operating Factors

Sales and marketing process—emphasize revenue generation … don't cut here.

Production operations—plan and demand effectiveness and efficiency.

Human resources management—stay lean and use overtime if needed.

Long-term trends—be aware of the limitations of talent and critical skill sets.

Accounting and Financial Factors

Interpretations of accounting statement data—use these tools effectively.

Financial condition and outlook—don't expect too rapid a recovery.

Long-term trends—keep debt and reserves at prudent levels.

Business Law and Tax Factors

Corporate governance—watch for changes and assure compliance.

Litigation issues—new problems may arise ... beware.

Government regulations and taxes—use all available provisions to conserve cash.

Long-term trends—don't expect some temporary regulations to ever be dropped.

Capital Market Factors

Level of inflation (or deflation)—know what to expect and the financial impact it will have.

Cost of debt and equity capital—read the text on this topic and minimize your debt.

Level of investment risk—assess and reassess the known areas of risk.

Long-term trends—project and integrate these into all uses of capital.

You can survive through a seemingly debilitating business crisis. To do that and get the best short-term gains without negatively effecting longer-term results, really think about how each of the listed factors will impact your three types of plans. (Plans to help you Survive, Build a Foundation, and Thrive.). Develop your survival plan by thinking about and ranking the amount of influence these different factors will have in the short-term. As you move on to your foundation building period and thrive plan development, appreciation of the longer-term waves creating these factors must be considered.

CHAPTER 3

TAKE ONE CAREFUL STEP AT A TIME

What's the Best Way to React in a Distressed Economy?

The previous chapters provided initial thoughts on surviving in an economic crisis. Once the business is stabilized and the move toward thriving is addressed, consider these thoughts below from noted business experts.

There are two schools of thought when times are tough and the future is uncertain. One says that businesses should cut expenses and prepare to ride out the economic storm. The other says that the period of disruption may be the best time to take positive steps and prepare for brighter days ahead. **A combination of both really is the best strategy**. In bad times, businesses in general should cut expenses and terminate marginally productive employees. (These are hard decisions to make. But they are both needed and important.) Now may be the time for you to take these actions unless there are overriding reasons via a government program or a future skills gap that must be addressed.

Let's take a look at some cost-saving measures that may provide the funds to build for the day when the distressing economic period is over.

Facilities

If you want and need some cash flow relief, ask for a ninety-day "rent holiday." (Offer to make up the rent over an eighteen-month period.) If your cash flow permits and you need commercial space for your future plans, now may be a good time to talk to your landlord about a favorable extension of your lease or some leasehold improvements.

Focus on things that might help the business provide better services, and so on. If the business is easily movable and your current lease is nearly up, make a move now to obtain favorable lease terms. Or, perhaps you have too much space. Try to convince the landlord to take it back, revise the lease, and deduct the rent currently due. Your objectives are to ask for help to survive and to optimize the space needed to thrive.

Operating space expenses have a direct bearing on your cash flow break-even point. Lowering these expenses will improve the foundation building picture and buy you time to implement your thrive change plans.

Insurance

Check into your medical and other insurance coverages. The cost is going nowhere but up; however, many insurers offer money-saving options. For example, a higher deductible may greatly reduce your premiums. Economically distressed periods are good opportunities to take a look at all your insurance programs, to reduce costs, lower your cash flow break-even point, and to better match the coverage with risks you have. Put your insurance agents to work for you.

Vendors

Talk to your largest suppliers. Maybe they are willing to give you a better break on price or terms now that they see you as a survivor. In a down market, they need business and will want to solidify their customer base. Ask for an early payment discount of 4% or 5% if your anticipated cash flow permits. These types of terms can put you ahead of the competition and keep you there. (Every small increment in increased margins boosts your survival quotient.)

Your leading vendors can also be an excellent source of up-to-date market knowledge. Be sure to ask for their input and whether they can provide low-cost or no-cost marketing or advertising support. They want you to succeed so you can pay them and help them grow over time.

Financial Processors

If your business accepts credit card purchases, speak to the bank that processes them for you. See if they will reduce the percentage they take. Offer discounts to your customers for cash payments if it makes good sense.

Drive Down Costs and Accentuate Growth Investments

Take a look at all your expenses. Can you cut them by ten percent or more without really affecting your business? After you have considered all of the above suggestions, turn your thoughts toward the positive side. Maybe now is the time to take aggressive measures to increase business revenues. After all, your competition is cutting back and downturns do not last forever. By reacting positively, your business may not only improve today, it will also have a head start on tomorrow. (These steps assume you can get an early indication on how to reposition your business in a changing marketplace.)

Some Proactive Measures

Here are some proactive measures to integrate into your three plans.

1. Increase your targeted advertising.

You can probably get good advertising deals in a slow economic period, so here is your opportunity to increase market penetration. Challenge your staff to find and use low-cost, no-cost marketing methods. Don't let anyone forget that the digital age is here. Press for effective and creative uses of all marketing channels with an emphasis of "online" activities. (This effort toward on-line sales and the resulting changes may become big parts of any corporate repositioning you might undertake as you develop your longer-term marketing plans.)

2. Emphasize service and quality.

In your advertising and in your marketing across the board, remember that the key to survival for many small and mid-sized businesses is service. By emphasizing quality and service, your business will not only survive in a recession, but will boom in the good times as well.

3. Hire if you need to.

If you need a crackerjack salesperson or another key employee, do not be reluctant to hire one now. There are always plenty of good people out there who are unemployed or underemployed in a depressed market. Also, do not forget about that whole group of talented (but inexperienced) college graduates searching for jobs in an inhospitable marketplace. By hiring that much-needed salesperson or key technical person, you will give your business just the jump-start it needs to stay on the road to survival and success!

4. Aim to fill a carefully defined niche.

Every advisor tells you to do this. Now is the time to find your niche! The bigger businesses get, the more voids they leave. When large businesses cut back, they produce even more and bigger holes in the business-world fabric. Change and expand your business to fill one or more of those holes.

5. Consider adding a new product or service.

Once you are operating at cash flow breakeven, it may be the moment to add a new product line or service. Every company in a difficult market is looking for new business. You may be able to strike a uniquely favorable arrangement with new suppliers. (Ask for special terms to build inventory without impacting your cash flows.) If you can do this, you will also be a step ahead of competitors who are waiting for the tide to turn.

Also, Could the Right Time to Buy Another Related Business Be Right Now?

"It was the best of times; it was the worst of times." Dickens was referring to a revolution instead of a temporarily disrupted economy or a longer recession. His words are still a good tagline for a disrupted independent business scene.

When you look back at a particularly difficult time, it may well go down in history as the era when investors should be buying small-to-medium-sized businesses. Maybe the best reason yet to look at a business combination is to add changes in order to survive. The fact that business prices are and may stay depressed for a while should not be the driving factor. You want to look only at ways to add to your product line and/or marketing strength. (However, do not neglect to fully assess all the factors outlined in other chapters.)

If you are considering or need to move into a business model with an emphasis of online sales or "virtual service delivery," acquisition of a struggling company with the needed human resource assets and technical attributes may be in order. This is the standard "buy or build" debate.

You may be able to accomplish an acquisition with little or no cash if you are willing to take a target's debt position. (You might even be able to negotiate with their lender to take over the debt at a discount if you can pay part of it down.)

Do not expect there to be much commercial financing available beyond survival support. When it comes to seeking acquisition financing in difficult times, by far the best sources are friends, relatives, and your business "networking" contacts. You can find more about how to approach an acquisition as a thrive strategy in Appendix C.

PART 2

REINVENTING AND INNOVATING
... A LITTLE OR A LOT

The "primary asset" you can use to survive and thrive is your ability to reinvent your business to take full advantage of the newly developing market realities and opportunities.

CHAPTER 4

LEARN FROM THE PENN CENTRAL BANKRUPTCY

The bankruptcy started when leadership decided they were in the railroad business ... instead of the transportation business.

While Penn Central was trying to run a railroad, people in other companies were inventing ways to employ trucks and planes ... to move people and things.

There is nothing so critical to the performance and success of a business as the correct perception of what that business is and how it relates to the market. That statement is worth repeating: There is nothing so critical to the performance and success of a business as the correct perception of **What that business is** and **How it relates to the market.**

And ... that is never truer than in the middle of a massive disruption of the marketplace! Understanding the purpose of your business may be the most important result you get from the painful, but necessary, crisis assessment of your business.

Here are a few examples of this required understanding: Hotels are not actually in the business of selling hotel rooms. A hotel room has a bed and a TV. It costs over two hundred dollars a night. But the business is much more than renting a room. Hotels are multi-million-dollar investments in hospitality and fine dining. They provide assurances of quality, efficiency, and genuine friendliness. And they should be marketed as such. That was the hotel business. Now ... keep your eyes open to see what hotels do to reposition their offerings after they are impacted by major health concerns and a dramatic decline in the flow of "traditional revenue."

Another business we all know rents cars. In an effort to move forward, they could move out of the rent-a-car business and into the travel and sightseeing business with an emphasis on health and safety. Through a merchandising, public relations, and marketing program designed to position such a company as **more** than a set of car keys and a rental car form, the company could become number one in a unique segment of the market.

Retailers will find the need for this type of thinking. Some will learn they were not in the dress business, but the personal fashion and service business. Others may recognize that they are not in the furniture business but in the interior home design business. And all retailers may find different ways to market with virtual tools and to rapidly expand online strategies.

The point is
before **you market what you are,**
you must *know* what you are.

Then, it becomes a matter of telling people what you are. This requires advertising, marketing, and public relations, using both traditional and newer methods.

Positioning your business for success will help you, first, increase your chance of survival in a crisis and, second, improve the long-term profitability of *your* business once the market recovers.

And, by the way, it turned out that Penn Central wasn't even in the railroad business. They were actually in the real estate business.

So as a business owner ... it is imperative to step back and determine exactly what business you are in. Is your business a manufacturer of a certain type of parts ... or are you really in a "service" or simply an "assembly solutions" business?

Knowing this ... is the first step to redeploying your assets to address the market as it changes in good times and bad. But it is more important in times of trouble because there may be no second chances to find the opportunity match for your business.

It may not be easy or immediately evident ... but as you can see from the history of Penn Central, knowing what business you are in—or should be in—makes a critical difference. Not knowing puts you at ever-increasing risk!

As the result of massive changes around you, this one assessment and revelation can make all the difference in the plans you develop. You should put this new knowledge in place to gain solid footing for your future. Include it directly in your foundation and thrive plans. So, before you start planning, sit down and think through what business you should be in to survive and thrive in the next few years.

CHAPTER 5

REPOSITION TO INCREASE EFFECTIVENESS

Let's take another look at this question about what business should you be in today ... and why!

Here is another broad industry example to set up the "repositioning" picture and burn it a little deeper into your mind. In normal times, every spring, the major cruise ship lines offer what are known as "repositioning cruises." These are special, extended cruises that offer the vacation seeker a long cruise at a bargain price. These "repositioning cruises' were not offered to attract customers but are part of the normal seasonal relocation of cruise ships so as to take advantage of better weather in different parts of the world.

So, before hurricane season hits in the Caribbean, the cruise lines reposition their ships to the Mediterranean where the weather is better, and demand is stronger.

And when the weather in the Mediterranean gets cold, the ships are relocated back to the Caribbean.

Do you want to operate your business in a massive "market equivalent" of a hurricane or do you want to find the sunny weather? It is all a matter of strategic positioning—using assets in the best possible way.

Seasonal repositioning was a normal part of the cruise business before the health scares that almost killed their businesses, so, can you imagine what types of discussion major cruise lines had to have when their businesses were shut down by the outbreak of a disease that was no fault of theirs ... but stopped all customer activity? The least of their concerns would be a potential hurricane that they might be able to steer around. They had to look at what amount of business revenue they could generate. What could they do to gain attention to what they offer and how do they convince customers to trust them? You must do the same thing!

Fortunately, few businesses have this type of extreme business disruption for the length of time that the cruise industry must anticipate after a health scare. But the question remains. How should you first define your business and then how can you effectively reposition it in a vastly changed marketplace?

It is time to use "Repositioning" as your personal PASSPORT to SUCCESS.

Every business owner must think about this and consider the benefits of repositioning their business to address directly or to create new market opportunities. This is the critical recurring process of planning to move from where you are now to where you want to be.

A small example might be to totally eliminate all inventory in a particular product group from a vendor. This might be done to radically change offerings or to reduce the number of vendors so you can concentrate your purchasing power. When you are making such a dramatic change you might sell the inventory you are holding at cost. Then use those funds to reposition your future offerings or to shore up your balance sheet.

Clearly, any actions in current inventory can contribute to both your survival plans and your foundation building phase. Actions here should help you prepare for the development of a new "picture of your business" for the future and provide cash flow in the near term.

Do not go too deeply into your planning until you make a full assessment of what business you want to be in "tomorrow" while the marketplace continues to transform. To do this, to accomplish your repositioning, you may have to, at times, drastically change daily business operations. The scope of your transition may shock many of your customers and employees, but those who have a greater understanding of today's business pace will know that it is just a part of your evolutionary drive.

You may have products or services that you do not want to handle in a changed marketplace. So, consider putting those parts of your business up for sale. (Do it carefully, confidentially, and with the right advisors.) You may not know who would be interested in buying the product group and the associated inventory. For someone with the right complementary product mix, your product group can be one of the keys to resurrecting their business.

When it comes to choosing a potential buyer, you want to sell the product group or service offering to someone who already knows it to avoid delay and to put cash in your pocket. The ideal buyer would be someone who has the ability to add your products to their existing operation. They can integrate and value the acquisition much more easily if they will only incur variable costs to add additional revenue If the new owner knows the market segment and what customers expect, it will it easier to negotiate an equitable price.

You want your cash out of the assets, but the potential margins the new owner can generate should control the asking price. It is best to get some professional valuation advice before you act. Understand you are selling a business unit not a collection of inventory assets. Price it that way!

With some effort and understanding of the task and its benefits, you may even find a buyer with a significant degree of synergy through increased purchasing power.

With thought and planning you will see how your product group or service offering can immediately benefit a buyer and their customers. Trust your instincts on this! Pick your spots and take actions with confidence.

This step reduces your scale of activity so you can eventually focus on higher priority tasks. But, maybe more importantly, the cash generated will buy you precious time to do the needed repositioning of your business while the marketplace changes.

These opportunities, uncovered when you know "what business you are really in," will create huge benefits for you and your operation for the long term. This is a critical preparatory step to your planning. It is one of the indispensable actions that will permit you to develop the solid foundation needed to create a thriving business.

CHAPTER 6

DO YOUR MARKET RESEARCH

Major corporations routinely spend hundreds of thousands of dollars on expensive and elaborate market research studies designed to help them better understand target markets and how their products are or should be positioned. These research projects often include mail and online surveys, telephone interviews, and focus groups. They take time and may not truly uncover the information to help management make better, quicker decisions.

Entrepreneurs running smaller businesses know that they also must acquire good market information to enhance their business development. Due to perceived costs and time requirements, this market research is often "deferred." This can lead to constant worries that management will not know how to reach their prospects and will not produce more profitable sales. These worries may be well-founded, but they do nothing to solve the problem.

The question is this: How do smaller companies gain the market knowledge necessary to effectively compete and grow today? In normally good times and bad!

For many smaller businesses, the cost of even one study from one of the big market research companies, let alone the recurring reporting really required, would exceed their entire marketing budget for a year or more. In addition, there is well-placed concern that the professionals from such firms will miss the mark and not sufficiently focus the efforts to provide the marketing insights the business owners are seeking.

The good news is that focus groups and other involved formal market research studies can be completely unnecessary if small company owners think about what they are really trying to accomplish. It is certainly possible to ask, "How can I better understand my current and future customers and the markets they operate in?"

Little time-consuming market research is required, because you should already know these things about your current customers, and you can learn about your prospective customers. Your business is succeeding at some level and delivering part if not all of what the customers want. You would not have acquired the current level of sales with them without delivering benefits they value. Even if you have not precisely formulated what this is, you probably know more than you think and can certainly ask a select group of customers a few simple questions to get them talking about "Why they do business with you today."

(As you do that, look for what it is that they "believe" about themselves, their company, their customers, and their market. Think about what it is that they "desire" to have happen each day. Ask how they are "feeling" about themselves and their actions in the marketplace.)

Trust yourself and your marketing team. You know more than you think you do ... and are closer to learning additional information that can make the difference as you design your marketing plans and develop new products for the future.

Management research has shown that many if not most decisions are driven by emotions and then justified analytically. (Think about the last few larger decisions you made. How did you really make them? And what did you do to "confirm" your decision?)

This can all be done with only a small amount of money spent on market research as long as the company constantly works to understand current and future customers. This same method can be applied to new markets by determining the answers to these questions: Who are the decision makers? Who are the key influencers? Then figure out what they believe in, what they really desire for themselves and their companies, and how they feel about the various personal and market relationships they encounter daily.

As the market changes, continuous improvement in collecting and organizing market and customer information becomes more critical. Seek to understand: What do they want? and Why do they want it? By uncovering new trends, every small business owner can add the information necessary to make better marketing and sales decisions.

CHAPTER 7

DEVELOP NEW MARKET KNOWLEDGE

O bviously, different is better than me-too. The question is not whether or not to be different, but rather how to communicate those differences in a way that customers will believe. The real challenge resides in market knowledge that can be used to an advantage. To understand good market research and development of market intelligence, the business owner should realize three things.

These three things are true, regardless of the state of the industry your business is in.

1. All businesses do the same thing: *They Attract and Serve Customers.*
2. All customers want just one thing: *The Best Possible Deal.*
3. Your marketing should do just one thing: *Articulate Why You're The Best Deal for Your Target Customer Segment.*

This is not complicated. If this is such simple stuff ... then why do most businesses have so much trouble marketing? It is because, in general, **businesses are poor collectors of market knowledge and even poorer communicators on these critical differences!**

Surprisingly, very few businesses really make more than a token attempt to distinguish themselves from their competitors. This is true partly because they have not made an effort to know the meaningful differences.

Fortunately, a business can cash in on what its competitors are doing both right and wrong. To get ahead of the pack, "Business Knowledge" must be sought and analyzed on a continuing and consistent basis.

Market research is a critical function within any organization. Today the term has broadened to "business intelligence." To succeed, every business should endeavor to learn "What it needs to know" and figure out how to acquire that information in a timely manner. In a crisis, use what you know and add to it before you make major marketing shifts.

Strategic Learning, a great book by William G. Pietersen, suggests that your research on markets and market segments should begin by you answering the following questions. Answer all these questions twice, first, to describe the conditions before the business disruption and second, to provide your best estimate for those conditions after the problems begin to subside.

1. How big is the pie? *(What is the estimate of the market size in dollars and key potential customers?)*

2. How big is the current slice of the pie held by your company? *(Dollars or number of key customers.)*

3. Who has the biggest slice of the pie? *(Who is the market segment leader in $ terms?)*

4. What is the current market leader doing right?

5. What might this market leader be doing wrong?

6. Who has the second largest slice of the pie? *(Answer questions 4 and 5 for them also.)*

7. What are the strategies that have been adopted by these top two market segment leaders?

8. How does your company measure up, in terms of dollars and numbers of key customers, strategy execution, and so on?

9. What can your company strategically do next to become the leader in the market segment?

10. How long will it take to become the market segment leader as you define leadership?

As information is developed and organized on any market segment, it should become truly clear:

1. Who are the *key customers* in the market segment?

2. Who are the actual *end users* of the products provided by these customers? *(Who is the ultimate driver of the extended purchasing process?)*

3. Who are the *decision-makers* in these companies?

4. Who are the *key influencers* in each of these companies?

5. Are there other *critical supporters of decisions* inside these companies? Who are they?

6. What do these end users, decision-makers, influencers, and critical-decision supporters value most?

7. Who is currently providing this value for them?

8. Is this supplier providing the desired level of value (benefits)?

9. How are the key customers' current suppliers assuring the delivery of value? (*What are their strategies and tactics?*)

You want to answer all these questions as you begin the critical planning for your business's future. This knowledge is a controlling input for your repositioning and strategy adoption. Simply write this information on a blank sheet of paper or use the **Survive and Thrive Workbook** you can find at

www.RichMowrey.com/Survive

The development of business intelligence is a process that should have the highest priority within any company. Every employee can contribute to the collective market knowledge. Little bits of information add up and help to complete the picture of "What is happening?" and "Why is it happening in this certain way?" each day in the marketplace. Armed with superior knowledge, your business can effectively develop strategies and tactics to meet or **exceed customer expectations** and **outcompete the competition**.

PART 3

FUNDING FOR TODAY AND TOMORROW

To break through to the "bright blue sky," you will need to properly finance your business.

CHAPTER 8

MAKE FRIENDS WITH YOUR BANKER

Banks are by far your best source for debt funding. They typically will provide the lowest interest rates and reasonable terms on loans. Your banking relationship may be the critical, deciding factor in a market catastrophe. Having the right relationship with your bank should help you to structure extended terms for loans and to open up a larger line-of-credit to cover working capital needs. In difficult times, the mix of loans and terms may require adjustments to meet your most pressing requirements. A good banking officer will understand the mutual benefit of accommodating your requests when they are based on solid analysis and plans.

When banking officers review and assess all of your cash flow planning, they should provide some advice, and can become trusted advisors. They are risk-adverse so their inputs will be on the conservative side. Just understand that fact and position your requests and interactions accordingly.

Bankers will be interested in your analysis of your cash flow break-even point. This analysis may help you to be successful in asking for a change in the terms of any outstanding or new debt. Consider using longer amortizations with balloon payments in five to seven years. These changes will positively contribute to the cash you will have available for reestablishing your foundation and generating growth.

As you craft your survive and thrive plans, search for the optimal combination of funding sources. Banks are your foundation but are not the only source of capital. Do not stop your financing search if your first efforts are not productive. Keep working on your plans until you have some assurance that the cash will be in your hands when you need it to stay on track.

CHAPTER 9

STAY FRIENDS WITH FRIENDS AND FAMILY

In most cases, friends and family are not the optimal sources of operating funds for any number of good reasons. But when you need small amounts of high-risk equity to start a business or to keep your business afloat, they are often the best sources.

If they have the funds and believe in you and your business, they can act quickly when time is of the essence. This is just what you must have in a cash flow emergency. So, if your survival depends on it, ask your friends and family for precisely what you need to survive. Make them a deal that you can live with and one you can follow through on. Allow enough time for you to actually develop the funds to pay them back or to buy back the stock issued. Do not make any promises that will be hard to keep in the next several years. (Distressed markets have an oversized element of the unknown. Both you and the person you are asking for funds should recognize this fact.)

Debt, in the form of a loan, may be the terms you use for discussion. Just know that these funds will be the equivalent of equity, since they will have no call on the company's assets. Do not let anyone think you are making them a partner unless you really are, and they can contribute. You do not need the distractions and they do not need the heartache.

Make sure you want to go down this path before you start. If it is the right choice, make the best advance you can and keep it as businesslike as possible. Be as transparent as you can be about the business needs for the funds. Advise the "investor" how and when you will update them on the progress you expect to make once you have the funds.

How much can you ask for from a friend or a member of your family? That depends on their personal financial position. If they have a business, you might approach them with an arrangement that involves that business. The size or the strength of their business will dictate the amount that can be invested. Try to have a good idea about their company's assets, debt structure, and value before you make an inquiry.

If the source has personal funds, you will want to have some understanding of their total assets. Try to ask for no more than 5% to 10% of their total assets. At that level, it will not be an insignificant a decision for them.

But, in that range, it should not impact their lifestyle or future prospects. You do not want to financially impact a person in your family or a close friend beyond that limit. You can certainly combine "loans" from multiple members of this group. It is normally best, however, not to mix friends, as investors, with family members who provide funds. No matter how hard you try, there will always be a difference between family and friends. Even if you make every effort to communicate effectively and treat everyone evenhandedly, there is too much risk of a misunderstanding when you have both friends and family as funding sources.

Do not ask for funds if the person has to take them from a retirement vehicle. Those funds are for retirement and not investments of this nature. You might find the need to "tap" your own retirement funds, but that big decision is only going to impact you. So, even if they offer, do not accept funds that cross this line.

CHAPTER 10

PARTNERS WITH MONEY

There are more Private Equity Groups (PEGs) active in the market today than in past years. Depending on how you define and count these investors, there are now over 3,500 active professional participants of this type in the US. These groups primarily invest in the private middle market.

Most Private Equity Groups have preferences for investments in specific industries. This is their first screen to determine if they have any interest. The target industries for the more active PEGs are well known within the merger and acquisition community. Part of the service provided by top middle-market acquisition advisors is effective management support of their investments.

Private Equity Groups rarely want to invest in businesses that are losing money. They are not turnaround specialists. However, if you had a strong financial performance before a crisis and have found a cash flow break-even footing, they may talk to you. A formalized plan will be a big help in facilitating useful discussions. If you speak to someone in this funding group that does not have a good match for your needs, they still may be able to refer you to someone with the required investment profile.

These investment groups are sophisticated business buyers with billions of dollars. But they have a big problem—they have far more capital than workable deals. They cannot find enough companies that fit their acquisition criteria to effectively deploy all of their available capital in good times ... let alone in a down economy.

The private investment groups' problems are greatly increased in times of economic distress when few companies are developing any notable measure of financial performance. They are frustrated and hungry, but they are disciplined. They normally have a strict minimum-size-company criterion for initial equity investments in a market segment. But they can be highly creative with preferred stock or convertible note investments in a highly disrupted market.

One standard investment approach utilized by PEGs is a corporate recapitalization. This is a popular technique when the owner wants to gain some liquidity, stay with their business, and benefit from the future growth of the company. In a distressed period, the approach permits the sale of a portion of the company at a price you might not accept in good times. But if it provides capital and a strong partner to help you manage through an uncertain future, a partial sale may make sense. It also will give you an opportunity to benefit if and when the company thrives in the future.

Some PEGs will do minority recaps. Some require control. Some will take equity directly and some will deploy a combination of convertible notes, preferred stock, and warrants. These terms are important but not as important as finding the right partner to help you manage your company. These professionals are also highly effective at arranging commercial financing once the company and the market reach a more "normal" position.

There is no easy way to make this critical decision.

Many owners hesitate and wait too long to move through all possible funding source discussions. In addition to the risks associated with such a delay, hesitation may inadvertently communicate a lack of confidence in the business. If necessary, engage an outside advisor who is familiar with the PEGs who are active in your industry to help with the process.

In summary, if you need a strong partner and a solid addition to your equity capital, you should consider this potential source of funds.

CHAPTER 11

RETIREMENT FUNDS

What if you could rescue your business with your IRA or 401(k) funds? Did you know that business buyers have occasionally been able to use their IRA or 401(k) funds to buy a business and not pay taxes or penalties at the time of the transaction? Since this is an accepted business transaction structure, you can potentially mirror it to gain access to the funds you need. There are creative ways to access retirement funds. This action will essentially move all or part of the ownership of your company into the retirement fund as an asset.

You need a specialist to make this happen, but it can be done at times with minimal cost!

There are many, many rules and, of course, some exceptions. If done properly, however, you can basically use your own retirement funds, tax-free, to fund your business. Be sure to engage your legal and accounting advisors in all of these investigations and decisions. Retain a specialist to make sure your plan qualifies, then follow these few key steps.

The mechanism works this way. There is a fee in the $5,000 range required to set this up. Also filing and other fees of approximately $1,500 and a small annual management fee will be incurred to assure future regulatory compliance. However, when compared to losing your company this option should be considered.

It sounds simple, but careful legal, tax, and technical navigation are critical to ensure that you do not violate any IRS rules that would result in a substantial penalty. Done correctly, this technique can unlock your retirement investment funds for use!

You will need a "corporate entity form" to accomplish this. Be certain to discuss this with your legal advisor and have it set up properly. Tax laws change and there may be other options permitted or regulations added.

The "Expert" that assists you will help with the establishment of the needed accounts and structure. Take a little time to investigate this funding source. If it will work in your situation, take the added time to complete the process with professional assistance. If it does not seem promising, move on to other options.

PART 4

REVISITING BASIC PRINCIPLES

REMEMBER YOUR MOST IMPORTANT ASSET

ow should a business owner answer the question, What is the biggest asset of your business? The answer really becomes elementary when you ask this additional question.

Can a business exist without customers?

So, as customers come back to your business after any type of disruption, you must double your efforts to meet their expectations. And ... their expectations may have substantially changed. They may be much more sensitive to how you approach filling all their needs, including safety and security, not just delivering a product or service.

It is crystal clear that how your CUSTOMER RELATIONSHIPS are reestablished after a business interruption will make or break your recovery. Customers, old and new, are and have always been the foundation of your business ... so never, never treat them like a commodity ... unless you want them to do the same to you. Every customer must be seen as unique and special. It is critical to recognize that fact and act accordingly.

Your customer relationships are going to be the number one asset you have to rebuild your business. By and large they will want to help you. So, focus on what should be done to develop and enhance your customer relationships. Help them help you by doing all of the following.

Constantly Communicate. Whether you communicate by email, text, Facebook, internet posts, telephone, snail mail, or in person, all your customers want to feel that they are special and that you will take special interest in seeing to their needs. (If you do not have an effective digital communication system, now is the time to set one up.)

Establish a Post-Purchase Reassurance System. Each time a customer places an order with you, follow up after he or she receives your product or service to see how it is going. This will reduce any post-purchase concerns and provide great feedback to foster improvement and changes if needed. (If you have not been doing this, this modification in your patterns will be noticed and appreciated by your customers. It can be the "edge" you need to generate recurring business in tough market conditions.)

Special Treatment. Give your clients the best deal. Give them absolutely no reasons to have any future pricing, quality, or service issues or concerns. This may be difficult when there is a high degree of uncertainly! But it is still required!

Preferential Pricing. Let your "old" active customers in on the best deals first. Give them the opportunity to buy your sale items before the public does. But do not stop there. Look back in your files and find those customers you lost and contact them. This may be a unique time to get them back as customers, especially if you can offer them something special. Research shows there is a much lower cost to reestablish a lost relationship than to find and gain a new one.

In your foundation planning, include a large measure of serving old and current customers in your tactics. These folks can help you generate revenue faster with fewer costs. Be conservative but persistent in this effort. Set goals for sales to particular groups. Assign responsibility to individual managers and work until you generate the break-even volumes you are seeking.

Build Trust. Be as transparent as you can be with your customers. Be clear about what you know and do not know. People want to and will do business with ethical people they can trust.

Today's technology provides great opportunities to develop and keep a current, updated customer list. Updating and reusing your customer list is crucial. If you do not have a solid system to track and communicate with your customers put one in place immediately and automate it

Know Your Customers. If you have a solid customer list, you can analyze it to figure out how to solidify your core customer base. Work with your existing and past customers to create a new business foundation. They've purchased from you before and if they had a good experience, they will buy from you again. Set up the communications systems necessary to make sure your customer knows why you are different ... why your products and services are different ... and why you can uniquely and consistently deliver to them the "best overall value"!

Remember the Golden Rule
(Do unto others ... .)
Your company should be run and operated
as you would expect it to be ...
As If You Were the Customer!

This is always true ... but when you are exiting from a crisis, it is important to not only operate in this manner, but for your customers to immediately and fully understand that this has been and will always be your overriding management principle! (You must feel their pain and understand their needs and address them.)

CHAPTER 13

MAINTAIN CUSTOMER LOYALTY

Effective research is the key. Find out whatever your customers need, want, and value. Find out what they simply must have from their suppliers.

Once you start asking questions to get these answers, a clear picture will form fairly quickly. (If you cannot do this yourself, hire a specialist to do it for you.) You want to develop the better offer, better product, better service. But you cannot do that until you know what your customers value in a changed environment. You must know how they are going to measure whatever you or your competitors do for them.

Not only should you find out what your customers want, but you should assess the end uses of the products and services you provide. How do these services and products help them? (Do whatever survey you can as fast as you can.) Once you understand the customers' ultimate use of what you supply, you can begin to help them use it more effectively to achieve their goals. And, if you can help them achieve their goals, you will have gained a customer for life. Not only that, you will have likely gained a productive and profitable referral source as well.

If you are not sure what your top customers value, contact customers and propose offers and identify benefits to them. Measure their reaction. Adjust the offer as you continue to research your own customer base. As times change, it becomes more and more important to tap into your customers' new wants and needs.

> **You must always remember that customers ultimately want the same thing: They want the best deal ... period! But, they do not all define the best deal in the same way.**

It is your job to find out exactly how customers define the best deal and then give it to them. Once you do that, you are positioned to dramatically increase your daily and monthly revenues while you concurrently create customer loyalty.

Once you start this process, you must constantly communicate with your customers. Consistently give them more information on how to use your products and services; provide more knowledge, more value, and the complete reassurance that you are providing them with the best deal. Continuity of this message with continuous feedback to make any and all required changes over time is key to successfully enhancing your renewed and your long-term relationship with your customers.

Know who your customers will be as you rebuild your business and who you want to serve for the longer term. Track and trend customer retention and reorder patterns. Then set objectives for both of these measures as part of your thrive initiatives. Plan accordingly to apply limited resources to accomplish your objectives.

CHAPTER 14

MANAGE WITHOUT EXCUSES

**In the end, critical objectives are either
realized or not!**

I t is widely understood that uniform tracking of operating results is the fundamental function of all business reporting systems. That is never more important than in the middle of a crisis. You must know where you are and keep working on getting to where you want to be!

This function provides assessments of the results and reports the changes and balances in various accounts. There is always some delay in this monthly reporting. To assure that you are making progress, it is important to track a few key indicators. Make a short list of the drivers that deliver the desired results for customers and assess them daily or weekly. (Use a trending reporting system for every critical operating measurement. A trend reporting discussion can be found in Appendix A.)

Management accountability should be based on the variance of operating results from the original targets. This should be accomplished with uniform measurements. This approach is required to systematically recognize success and failure in a manner that immediately prompts analysis, acceptance of responsibility, and actions to foster improvement in real time.

When times are difficult, you do not want nor can you accept substandard performance. For example, if a company's total sales or regional sales do not meet its objectives, someone must be "accountable" for the actions or lack of actions that should have been taken to mitigate the variance from the sales for the period. There should be no attempt by managers to assign poor results to a declining economy or to a competitor's introduction of a new product. They should accept responsibility specifically for the variance from the planned sales results. Management's job is to produce the needed (planned) results ... period! (In bad times, management should step up and find solutions!)

Reporting on the circumstance of any variance is just that—it is not an analysis and not a way to off-load responsibility. If any part of your management team does not fully recognize and accept the responsibility for the company's results, they will always be looking for ways to assign away the variance instead of aggressively and creatively seeking corrective actions.

Never view management's job in such a manner that any performance gap can be ascribed to "uncontrollable forces" outside the company. **Justification dilutes accountability and hinders the development of required new knowledge.** One cannot view management's job as partly passive when it is convenient.

What counts, and the only thing that matters in the end, is the answer to this: Were the required objectives, especially in planned weekly cash flow, met or not? If not, why not? And what has and is being done to ultimately achieve the target performance objectives and recover the variances?

It must be understood that the lack of timely actions or the wrong actions is too often the basis for performance deficits. In the discussion here, if management knew or should have known that the economy, market, or customer preferences were changing, then it was their responsibility to react and act to still realize the planned objectives. True accountability comes from the knowledge of and the acceptance of responsibility for poor outcomes. Failure to step up for the company and the other employees is not acceptable, regardless of the reason(s).

It is this embracing of overall responsibility without "justification for poor results" that will deliver consistent, optimal performance. This is the type of management problem that can turn a difficult business disruption into a bankruptcy.

Conversely, a management team that always accepts responsibility and tailors actions accordingly can stand proudly on all outcomes in varying economies or competitive environments. It is the complete acceptance of responsibility that fosters continuous learning by management and ultimately makes the difference in strategy development and execution.

Management's (and the business owner's) ability to adapt to rapid and/or hidden changes will ultimately control the company's success or failure. Do not expect this attribute to be in place unless you highlight its value and reward actions accordingly.

A disciplined use of project responsibility assignment and tracking will help create the preferred management mindsets. Get a "buy in" from every team member on all project steps and objectives. Then help your team succeed each and every time.

CHAPTER 15

UNDERSTAND THESE PRINCIPLES

Unfortunately, we are all too often saddled with the news of hurricanes, floods, and earthquakes or pandemics. All of these "natural occurrences" can disrupt business activity. And, as we know, some businesses survive these situations with extra effort, and some do not!

We also all too often hear news of ongoing war(s). Regardless of how you feel about the strategy and tactics in these constantly occurring human-to-human "engagements," there are critical principles that apply to both war and management.

A working understanding of these time-tested principles from the fifth century can help you address the battles in your industry and in your business. *The Art of War* written by Sun Tzu makes it clear that information does matter. His thesis is that an educated guess is better than a gut decision. Sun Tzu thought that generals should be adept at using "military calculus." This is simply taking into account anything and everything that could affect the outcome of a battle. These principles are clearly applicable to business in general and to survival when the changing environment is awfully hard to understand.

Every Business Owner Should Review these Principles on a Regular Basis!

Develop all your plans and then manage daily activity based on an understanding of how each principle effects the performance of your business. If you do not have a large overriding measure of these principles "showing up" in your plans, they may not provide the path and results desired. As you craft all of your projects, be sure you apply these principles.

Objective. You must have a clearly defined and obtainable set of objectives.

(You must know where you want to go, measure progress, and understand the benefits of succeeding and the risks of different outcomes.)

Offense. Seize, retain, and exploit the initiative.

(To succeed, management must continuously "out market" and "out serve" the competition. When customers are starting to reestablish buying relationships, this is the difference maker.)

Mass. Concentrate forces at the decisive time and place. *(Know how and where to apply the strength and all the hidden assets of the company to the market place to provide benefits for the customer. Be sure to focus effort and limited capital to create a competitive advantage)*

Economy of Force. The mirror image of Mass—keep the minimum of force at non-critical points. *(Don't squander effort and assets on tasks with a low probability of success. Priority use of assets and personnel is a must in difficult times.)*

Maneuver. Don't be a sitting duck. *(Stay flexible, assess trends, and adjust plans in accord with changing information.)*

Unity of Command. Too many chefs spoil the broth. *(Leadership is critical; make sure the operating structure and management responsibility and accountability enhance the decision-making process.)*

Surprise. Do what they won't expect. *(Outthink the competition, be creative, learn to take measured, well-timed risks.)*

Security. Make sure they do not surprise you. *(Constantly research the market, systematically study customers and analyze the competition, and be prepared to handle any new developments quickly.)*

Simplicity. Complicated plans are a formula for disaster in the chaos of war.

(Carefully choose the right strategy, understand the critical elements for success, and plan accordingly.)

If all your plans and actions follow these principles, YOUR business will surely benefit and consequently survive in the short term and thrive in the long term.

PART 5

BEING CAUTIOUS

CHAPTER 16

PRICES—HOLD 'EM OR FOLD 'EM

t is normal and natural that price and value perspectives differ between buyers and sellers. A simple experiment highlights what is happening and can help us understand. It shows what occurs as the parties approach the transaction process. Here is one example that is taught in negotiation training.

Two groups of students are randomly selected. Each member of one group is given a cup and the members of the other group is not. The two groups are separated and not in contact with each other. The group without cups is independently shown a cup and asked what price they would pay for it. Their answers centered around $4. The other group, who had the cups in their possession, were each separately asked what they would take to part (sell) with their cup. These answers centered around $8.

Many experiments of this nature have been repeated with similar results. What is happening? It is human nature to value something "in our possession" higher than the same thing we do not have. Couple this basic human nature and it is no wonder that customers and suppliers have differences. The extent of this variance between the seller's price and the underlying market value is important to determine. If there is insufficient understanding of the value, then there will probably be no sale. Consequently, as a business owner, it is your overriding responsibility to communicate and deliver value.

It should always be remembered that As a buyer,

Price is what you pay and value is what you expect to receive.

Conversely, as a seller,

Price is what you receive and value is what you deliver.

Price negotiation between well-informed parties should result in a balance that the parties can maintain to foster a longer-term relationship. As the seller, you must position your product or service in the buyer's mind to have "real value." When you do that, you can ask for and receive good gross margins.

That is the basic picture of the market and the players. It should always be remembered that both you and your customer have perceived and real alternatives. However, if you want your business to survive and thrive, you must resist the impulse to cut prices. That is not to say that you cannot run a "promotional discounted product opportunity" occasionally. The key is a quick return to the needed level of gross margin required to run your business and to thrive.

Older, experienced, manufacturing managers often say when asked why they passed up a sale with very tight margins, *"I don't need any more practice in manufacturing!"* This means there is no reason to take an order without it having a sufficient contribution margin to make a meaningful impact on the bottom line.

Inexperienced sales personnel often argue for reducing prices. They are missing the understanding of the impact to operations and company profitability, **not to mention the message it sends to customers.**

Far too few managers understand the true cost of cutting pricing. This simple chart shows the required increase in sales for different "price discounts."

If the PRICE CUT is:	If Your Present Gross Margin is:			
	20%	30%	40%	50%
5%	33.3%	20.0%	14,3%	11.1%
10%	100.0%	50.0%	33.3%	25.0%
15%	300.0%	100.0%	60.0%	42.9%
20%	N/A	200.0%	100.0%	66.7%

The chart emphasizes the increase in units sold that are required just to break even for a given price reduction (that is discounts under various scenarios). This chart should drive the "price cutting" reality home. Use this chart to educate yourself and your managers. All businesses must work to maximize the gross margin generated. Without a focus on this measure and how price cutting impacts it, disaster may be close at hand!

Here is a quick summary on that point. When times are tough, it is all too common to reduce prices to maintain or to attract new customers. This should almost never be done. That is not to say that a properly structured promotion cannot be used within a larger strategy. If you are repositioning inventory or taking similar actions, that is a different set of pricing considerations. What we are discussing here is the high risk, negative results from "lowering" operating margins.

Here is an example to show why that subject is so important. If your gross margins are 40% and you reduce your prices by 10% you will need to increase the total number of units sold by 33.3% to generate the same margin dollars! Is that going to happen as you strive to survive a downturn? It probably will not happen even in good times, but it certainly will not be your reality in a slow market.

Please take a close look at the real cost of price cutting! The chart shows you how many more units, at the reduced price, you must sell just to earn the same gross margin you had before you cut the price. Do not drop your prices without utterly understanding what this table is showing you!

To avoid making this type of pricing mistake—Deliver value! Communicate that fact! Get the prices and margins every day that you need to both survive and thrive.

CHAPTER 17

RECOGNIZE DEBT'S REAL COST

Any time we enter a period of changing interest rates, some business owners may find debt financing to be increasingly attractive. Business owners often think that the only cost of debt is its stated interest rate. If you borrow $1,000 at 5%, you have to pay $50 in interest every year, and that's that, right?

No! Debt is much more expensive, for many reasons:

1. All businesses have to pay back the principal, too! Many people forget to include this after-tax payment in their calculations. Banks lend other people's money and have to be able to get it back! Many borrowers and lenders have forgotten this repayment risk to their detriment.

2. Use of debt financing may entail **loan covenants that restrict the borrowers' prerogatives** in areas such as compensation, capital expenditures,

dividends, and distributions. The interest rate does not reflect these costly limitations on control and ownership benefits.

3. A personal guarantee or other collateral is almost always required: THAT can be restrictive and hugely expensive when things go badly!

4. Additional reporting requirements *(audits, monthly statements)* can be costly, time-consuming burdens.

5. Other compliance requirements *(such as credit life insurance or asset appraisals)* add costs.

6. If the repayment schedule is inflexible and cash flow is barely sufficient or inadequate to cover current obligations, the risk of insolvency is material. *(In this case, the loan could be called, or placed in "workout," in which even more onerous controls are enforced).*

7. Today, some debt has floating interest rates pegged to the prime rate *(e.g. prime plus 2.5%)*. If interest rates rise, the cost of debt will rise accordingly.

8. Debt from non-bank capital firms almost always includes "equity kickers" such as stock options and warrants that can dramatically increase the cost of the financing package. Typical "mezzanine" financing has an overall cost of 15% to 18% *(including both debt and equity components)*, even though the debt component might have a stated interest rate of 8% to 10%.

Do not be fooled by the interest rate alone: the hidden costs of debt are far greater!

With this little tutorial in place, do not stop yourself from arranging whatever loans you need to survive, especially if the bank is offering uniquely attractive terms. Just, recognize that any future principal payments are after-tax disbursements of cash and that earnings must be correspondingly higher to be able to make those payments in a timely manner. You always want to borrow only the amount of funds you need to survive and eventually thrive. No more ... no less!

There are some alternatives to adding bank debt that may be able to drive your plans faster with less impact on future cash flows. These options may not be the best choices for you and your business, but an understanding of these approaches should help you develop optimal plans. Another look at the funding resource options presented earlier may be in order if your debt load is stacking up "too high"!

CHAPTER 18

UNDERSTAND AND PLAN CASH FLOW

We have been talking a great deal about the importance of "cash flow." Like many other financial terms, "cash flow" has many definitions, but it ultimately measures the tangible economic benefit of ownership (cash available for distribution) rather than "income" *(profit)*, which is an accounting and tax concept.

It is very important to always know how cash flow is defined. There are different measures of cash flow and at time bankers and others may use the term in a way you don't expect without defining it.

All business analysis starts with revenue, the proverbial "top line." Expenses are then deducted, arriving at earnings after taxes *(net income, the "bottom line")*. Along the way, two popular calculated "income measures" are developed: EBIT (earnings before interest and tax expenses) and EBITDA (earnings before interest and tax expense and before depreciation and amortization expense). Although some people think these two terms measure cash flow, they do not. They do not reflect balance sheet considerations such as working capital needs, capital investments, and debt service.

Profitable businesses fail if they run out of cash *because of demands for high working capital, large investments in fixed assets or high debt payments.* Cash flow calculations reflect changes in three sets of balance sheet accounts that do not appear on the income statement: working capital, capital expenditures, and debt service *(principal payments).*

Here are some measures of cash flow. The first is "Gross Cash Flow." It is aptly named. It does not reflect balance sheet changes or tell the analyst much. "Operating Cash Flow" another measure is helpful because it includes changes in working capital (receivables, payables, and inventories). Many profitable businesses get into "cash flow" difficulties when their receivables and inventories become excessive, tying up cash. **Operating cash flow is a good measure of viability and what you should focus on to plan through a survival period.**

"Net cash flow to equity" is the cash available to the owner(s) after capital expenditures are funded, loans are repaid, and new loans are taken out. This measures the amount of money available for distributions *(ignoring loan covenants).* This is often referred to as "free cash flow."

An "Increase (Decrease) in Cash" is the ultimate measure of business health. This is how much more or less cash the business will have after funding everything else. This is the real "bottom line." In recovery mode, the additions to working capital are the first priority. Do not plan on making any distribution or investing in new capital equipment in your first part of recovery unless it is critical to lowering operating costs or positioning for survival.

"Debt-Free Cash Flow" calculates the cash that would have been available to the owner(s) if the business had no interest-bearing debt. This is important in acquisitions in which only assets will be sold, and the buyer will establish a different financing structure. *(If you determine it is a positive step to sell off a product or service line, this is the benefit stream to understand for those discussions. Similarly, if you decide that it is a viable strategy to acquire another business in the near-term environment, this is the benefit you should be seeking to acquire.)*

There are three things to remember about all of this:

1. Each measure of cash flow reflects benefits accruing to different combinations of owners, creditors, suppliers, and so on.

2. Each cash flow measure has different risk characteristics. Sales, the grossest measure of activity, indicates nothing about profitability.

3. There is no general relationship between the magnitudes of profit and cash flow. Each business has its own characteristics.

**Please remember, before you engage in any
discussion of cash flow, be sure all parties
are working with the same definition.**

When You Do a Cash Flow Plan, Be Conservative!

There is nothing magic about cash flow planning. For
your survival plan, these initial projections should be
weekly for the first four weeks of the anticipated disruption period. Be conservative about inflows from funding
sources and normal operating elements. Your customers may be much slower to pay you than you could ever
imagine. Plan accordingly. Figure that many will only
pay you 50% of all outstanding invoices in this critical
period. (Assign a pleasant-voiced staffer to follow up and
ask for payment politely again and again ... until it is
your turn to call!)

Once you see the projected total cash that will be at
your disposal to survive this first four to eight weeks,
allocate the cash as per the discussion in chapter 1.
Here is that recapped with some added comments for
weekly planning.

- Payroll is always first. (Can you ask for some sal-
  ary deferral from top managers? Yes! Do this if
  needed.)

- Rent, insurance, and utilities are second on this
  hierarchy (Ask for some breathing room here so
  you can allocate this cash elsewhere as needed.)

- Local vendors should be paid within terms if at all possible.

- Key vendors can help you. Negotiate to survive and keep them as suppliers and the good friends they probably have become.

It is best to set up a weekly total cash outflow allocation amount and then to work with the priorities as you see them, and as new information develops. If you are fortunate to have more inflows than planned, do not be too quick to increase your planned weekly outflow amounts. The next week can be a surprise in the other direction.

Here is a simple outline for a cash flow tracking template for your survival period. (Your accounting advisor can support you with this if needed. Ask!

Set a cash-in-hand objective for the end of the fourth week. Try to stay on track. In a distressed market, there may be some panic among both customers and vendors. Be the calming voice. Ask for the flexibility you need. Keep on tract to have the targeted cash to start the second four-week portion of your survival plan. Budget out those weeks and apply the same principles and priorities. Look at the cash balances throughout this period on a daily basis. Make all critical adjustments with a clear head and the confidence that you will survive.

As you get to the end of the second four-week period, you should have your first year of recovery planning

	Beginning Cash Balance	Week 1	Week 2	Week 3	Week 4
Cash Balance					
Sources of Funds (Inflows)					
Acc't Rev'b Collection					
Asset Reduction Sales					
Inventory					
Fixed Assets					
Funding Sources					
Other					
TOTAL PLANNED INFLOW					
Cash Amount to ALLOCATE					
Cash Uses (Outflows)					
Payroll					
Utilities					
Insurances					
Rent (Leases)					
Local Smaller Vendors					
Key Major Vendors					
Other					
TOTAL PLANNED OUTFLOW					
CASH BALANCE @ WEEK END					
ALLOCATED Amounts NOT Paid					
Capital Equipment Purchases					
List the Vendors & Allocate Cash					

completed and updated along with a corresponding budget. Your budget work should include both income statement and balance sheet projections. Involve your outside advisors in this budgeting process. They are experienced professionals who are skilled in making projections. This is your thrive financial position and a picture you want to realize by the end of the first twelve to fifteen months.

That budget document should permit you to delegate the cash flow management to someone with the responsibility of maintaining the projected balance of cash inflows and outflows as you go from survival to building your new foundation for success. Do not get too far away from tracking and maintaining your personal awareness of the company's cash balances.

CHAPTER 19

AVOID WRONG STRATEGY COSTS

Too many managers are quick to choose a wrong strategy and too slow to recognize the costs associated with the execution of that wrong strategy. It pays to take a little more time to get on the right track and to then continuously assess the results against expectations. (Do not get hung up on the "business terms." Focus on the purpose of why your business exists and how you can best deliver value at the lowest possible cost.)

**The costs of choosing the wrong strategy
can be huge.**

There are Six Big Costs that can be avoided by taking the time and doing the research and thinking to establish the correct strategies in each business area. Take a look at the costs you want to avoid. Start right and finish on target and on time. Start wrong, fail to assess and change, and you will be dragged under by these Big

Six Costs, which are listed below. In good times, you may have a second chance. In an economic or individual business crisis, there are no second chances. You must adopt and exercise the optimal strategies for survival. You must avoid losing ground in the following ways.

1. By spending direct project-related expenses that do not provide the desired result. *(You can only spend it once.)*

2. By investing man-hours of effort (from all direct and indirect employees) to execute the failing strategy. *(In most businesses, this is the limited resource that must be applied in the right way at the right time.)*

3. By allowing frustrations and lost opportunities to affect a Return on Investments of time and money. *(Failed strategies can greatly affect the overall returns for shareholders and impact both CAP-X planning and compensation plans.)*

4. By underestimating the loss of chronological time needed to achieve desired goals and objectives. *(You can restart, but the clock does not ... so you will have to do double-time to reach the objectives as planned.)*

5. By losing your colleagues' and other management's confidence in your judgement. *(Once gone, it is hard to regain!)*

6. By impacting personal belief in your ability to predict results of implementing a strategy as well as losing faith that desired objectives can be realized. *(No manager can be effective unless he or she believes in their own abilities to make good decisions.)*

The last two of these costs may be the greatest, since they can take a toll long into the future, and impact personal and professional achievements that are critical to enhancing business performance. Reflecting on these costs of choosing the wrong strategy is a must before you finalize your survive and thrive plans.

PART 6

THRIVING PLANS

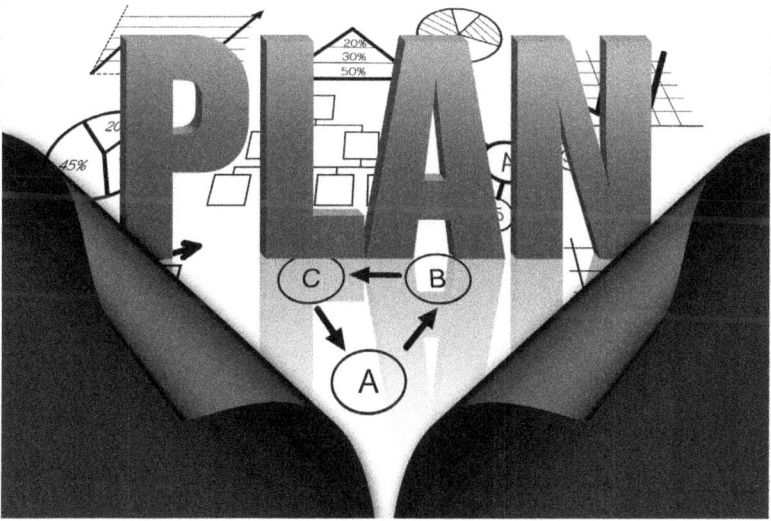

CHAPTER 20

PLAN THROUGH TOUGH TIMES

To get a jump start on the survival planning process, write down your best answers to these internal evaluation questions. You can find a workbook for easy use at:

www.RichMowrey.com/Survive

As noted before, you must think about the past when times were good and make your best estimate of what the near-term future holds. This picture of where you are and what your customers will want and need is going to be critical to your success. If your business has been closed or disrupted for a period of time by uncontrollable events, do your best to "see into the future." Get others with some added insight to help you if necessary. Do not be concerned if you think you have answered some of these questions before. Just jot down your best responses.

Here are the internal evaluation questions to carefully answer:

Who are your best customers? Why? (Will they come back? Stay?)

Who are your most difficult customers? Why?

Who are the key suppliers? How long have you done business with them?

Have you ever had any difficulty with your key suppliers? Explain the situation.

Who are your key employees? Why? Are there any issues concerning these employees ... now or in the past?

Who are the employees most critical to daily operations?

Who really does the sales work for the company? How much do you do?

What do you do every day? Who else can do the things you do?

Who runs the company when you are gone?

What do you like best about the business?

What do you like the least about the business? Can you change this?

How long do you think it will take for you to "train" new employees and managers with the critical skills to effectively run the business?

What should be done to build the business? Why hasn't it been done before?

What kind of problems do you have with the production processes?

When was the last time you lost a day of production due to such problems?

What kinds of problems do you have with the building?

When was the last time you had to address a major building problem?

What type of leases do you have for the operating transportation equipment? When are the leases up? What changes would you make in the new leases?

What worries you most about the business? What have you done about that?

Who are your primary competitors?' (What channels do they use to attract and deliver to customers? Who are their top five customers or customer groups? Who are their top five managers? Who are their top five vendors?)

What can they do that you and/or the business cannot or has not done?

How does the business stack up to the competition in the areas of Products, Prices, Service?

What can be done to improve your competitiveness? Why have you not done that?

Who does the purchasing of primary raw materials for the business?

Who sets the prices? Should this change in the middle of a crisis?

What causes prices to be changed?

How are price changes determined?

When was the last time prices were changed?

How were these changes implemented?

How often do you personally meet with customers? (Will your renewed customer base accept virtual visits?)

When was the last time you met with a top ten customer? What was the subject of the meeting?

What expansion plans do you have in place? Are they in writing? Do you have any quotes on building expansion plans or for new equipment?

When do you think it will be necessary or desirable to expand the production capacity?

Do not keep driving the "old truck" when your competitors may be preparing to move on in style in a new hybrid with more horsepower. Do not jump into new "in vogue" changes, but do not rule them out either. There is no secret that online business models are taking a larger and larger share of the total market. The question on this score should be this: How do the customers want to "shop"?

In or out of a business crisis … nothing matters more than having good customers. To paraphrase a noted political comment,

It is the Customer … Stupid!

Every business owner and every employee should constantly keep searching for information on the current and future customers ... and then applying the lessons learned.

By completing the answers to all of these questions, you should be on your way to developing solid information to feed into an innovative set of goals and objectives and the strategies to reach them.

CHAPTER 21

USE TRADITIONAL STRATEGIC PLANNING

I t is time to put this critical management process to work for you to build a thriving business.

Strategic Planning is defined as a process that uses the expertise of the internal management staff in the development of methods and plans to achieve goals for the company. Too many smaller businesses shy away from this process. There is nothing magic about it. Regardless of how you see the "term," we know that a planned operation outperforms an unplanned one by over 20 percent ... over and over again. So, let us lock in these well-established concepts and look at the planning approach as a tool for creating a thriving business.

Specific operating methods (strategies) devised during the planning process should focus use of resources (potentially limited by a distressed situation) of the organization in a way that addresses the opportunities available. These plans should be reduced to the achievement of specific measurable objectives that accumulate into a realization of the identified goals.

The strategic planning process is usually longer-term ... that is it uses a horizon of three to five years. Given that longer planning period, it is recognized that the plan in total will not be completed as drafted. This "capstone plan" should provide for the regular incorporation of new information and feedback. Such an approach should improve the strategies and establish additional objectives necessary to continuously move toward the supported goals.

So, do you need a longer-term strategic plan in the middle of an economic crisis? Yes, you do! You may not need nor should you take the time to do everything you might do in a more "normal" business environment. But the process is important to bubble up the proper business positioning, marketing strategies, and application of available resources.

There are many ways to segment the planning function. We have addressed a lot of the preparatory work and thinking required to develop the right plans for the conditions of your business. You can use that previous analysis to complete these "traditional" planning statements.

There is a FREE outline planning template available to you in the download area.

www.MergerMentor.com

Simply register for your FREE membership and then go to the download area. It is a fill-in-the-blanks PDF template. You can use it to guide you through the traditional planning steps. Just fill in the blanks to get a solid start on the needed foundation for all your plans.

(You can certainly also use other planning tools or engage an experienced strategic planner to help you develop your longer-term thrive plans.)

This template will lead you through the typically accepted processes, which are as follows:

- Develop a Mission Statement
- Develop Goals and Objectives
- Conduct a Comprehensive Needs Analysis
- Assess Available Resources
- Develop Strategies to Achieve the Goals and Objectives
- Establish Measures for All Objectives to Realize Goals
- Develop Action Plans (projects with a one-year time or less horizon)
- Develop an Assessment System (seek and use feedback loops)

To enhance the strategic planning process, it is helpful to understand the difference between goals and objectives. The chart below provides a quick way to compare and contrast these two important terms.

	Goal	Objective
Plan Type:	Broad Plan	Narrow Plan
Type of Action:	Generic Action	Specific Action; Specific Time
Measure:	Normally not directly measurable or tangible	Must be measurable and tangible
Time Horizon:	Longer-Term	Short or Medium Term
Understood Meaning:	The purpose toward which an endeavor is directed	Something that step-by-step actions are intended to specifically accomplish
Principle Involved:	Based on Ideas; Qualitative	Based on Facts; Quantitative

The word *Goals* has the word *Go* in it. The organization's goals should show the way forward in a specific direction.

Part of moving toward a goal is the benefit of what is accomplished on the journey.

The word *Objectives* has the word *Object* in it. Objects are concrete and physical. The organization's objectives must be clearly outlined with timelines, budgets, and personnel requirements, and have **measurable outcomes**.

Do not short cut this process. You do not have months to do it, but you need to take at least a few days to really do the research and thinking to get on the right strategic path. Remember the caution provided for your edification earlier on the costs of choosing the wrong strategy.

Sound STRATEGIC THINKING is critical to business success.

The strategies chosen will have the controlling influence on the successful accomplishment of any business plan. Consequently, it is essential to understand what strategy is and does ... and what it is not.

STRATEGY focuses on EFFECTIVENESS, which is doing the RIGHT THINGS. TACTICS by contrast emphasize EFFICIENCY, which is doing THINGS RIGHT.

Both are important but becoming more efficient in doing the wrong things will only waste time and resources. So, identify the right strategies and constantly test them to be sure they will maximize the "Return on Effort" (ROE) as well as the "Return on Investment" (ROI) inside your organization.

Sound Strategy development always demands more THINKING ... and better THINKING.

Your primary objective for the **Survive Plan** is to not run out of cash!

Your objectives for your **Foundation Plan** are going to incorporate a degree of the strategies and tactics identified in the Thrive Plan. This is a repositioning phase for your marketing and expense reduction to achieve cash flow break-even operating results ... at a minimum. Consequently, you need to know where you want to go after the first six months of survival work (that is, how to fulfill the company's purpose!).

The **Thrive Business Plan** should cover the balance of the first twelve or fifteen months. It should be formed around a crystal-clear picture of your business and a deep understanding of "what business you are and want to be in"! The optimal strategies you will discover in your planning work should build seamlessly on the new foundation you build.

Hopefully, you found the background information in the different chapters to be stimulating to your thinking. Here is a twelve-day timeline for rapid development of your three plans to ensure survival and to craft a durable, thriving period for your business.

Day		Actions-Planning Process Objectives
1	a.	Assemble Cash Flow Information (Account Balances, Inflows, Outflows).
	b.	Develop a first draft of your Cash Flow Survival Four-Week Plan.
2	a.	Start to investigate Funding Sources (Short and Long-term).
	b.	Begin the Rethinking, Repositioning Process as inputs to planning.
3	a.	Answer the Market Research and Competitive Intelligence questions.
	b.	Identify sound innovative steps to create a Competitive Advantage.
	c.	Draft some initial steps to implement changes to match the market.
	d.	Develop a breakeven analysis for your operation before any changes.
4	a.	Reassess your Cash Flow Plan with new information (deferrals, etc.).
	b.	Allocate cash resource to categories for the next four weeks.
	c.	Make any necessary short-term staffing decisions (furloughs/layoffs).
5	a.	Reassess the Repositioning with full consideration of Basic Principles.
	b.	Develop your first cut on your Changing Target Market Picture.
	c.	Create plans to sell assets if indicated (inventory, etc.).
	d.	Follow-up on Funding Sources (as needed short and long-term).
6	a.	Add internal analysis to your planning - SWAT, Marketing Worksheet.
	b.	Complete your expense reduction analysis (Cut 10% or more if possible).
	c.	Take a creative look at technology use to lower costs and add service.
	d.	Develop a revised break-even analysis with all known changes.

Day	Actions-Planning Process Objectives
7	a. Use the Brief Outline Planning Template to draft a Thrive Plan.
	b. Outline 4 to 5 major projects on the template to implement strategies.
	c. Communicate the plans and projects to managers and staff (seek input).
8	a. Create your Foundation Plan based on Cash Flow and the Thrive Plan.
	b. Modify the front end of major projects within the Breakeven limits.
	c. Put market information collection systems in place.
	d. Reassert who your key customers are and will be.
	e. Establish a superior customer care and communication system.
	f. Make all needed operating changes dictated by customer concerns.
9	a. Start to aggressively implement your customer "revival plan".
	b. Add communications to generate sales to current customers.
	c. Check and reaffirm pricing and margin strategies (be disciplined).
	d. Execute first step plans to attract new customer.
10	a. Access Funding Sources (Short and Long-term).
	b. Step back and look at short-term and long-term staffing needs.
	c. Implement a strategy to attract and retain all required skilled staff.
	d. Start a hiring process for newly required staffing to execute plans.
	e. Update your Survive Cash Flow plan to extend through eight weeks.
11	a. Establish the project due dates with required updated inputs.
	b. Reassess and execute assets sales and other Survival strategy steps.
	c. Complete initial CAP-X plans for six months (change driven only).
	d. Determine how to best fund CAP-X plans (cash, debt, or equity).
12	a. Solidify your Foundation Plan to integrate with the Survive Plan.
	b. Finalize your Thrive Plan (update the template) to guide decisions.
	c. Finalize your Projects for the near and longer-term actions.
	d. Put initial Trend Reporting in place to track and adjust activities.
	e. Make some tangential considerations of an acquisition's benefits.

CHAPTER 22

A SURVIVE-AND-THRIVE REMINDER

You now have a variety of planning suggestions and tools that will stimulate your thinking. The thinking required to fully address the new opportunities available in periods of accelerated change. All these should lead you to formalizing and completing the three required plans to survive and thrive. These plans are just that—plans. The actions you and your team take to execute them will make all the difference. Here are some reminders and prompts to help you finish your plans and to lean into this journey.

By now you may be weary of hearing about changing your business model to "match up" to the new market realities. Hopefully, repositioning and reinventing your business should have you excited. There are no guarantees! But it is guaranteed that if you do not fully assess where your business is and take action to meet the evolving market challenges you will not get the results you are seeking. So ... feel the fear and do it anyway!

Your newly developing business may need to shed assets, products, or product lines, and change in other ways. It may need some new and different human resources to drive future growth as you bounce back. So, work as needed to fully reestablish the business with the assets you have in hand.

The picture should be clear on what the business will be and will be doing. Your analysis should have revealed the answers to all of these questions.

- Who are the target customers and why?
- How will your business be positioned to have a competitive advantage?
- How will you market to these customers in new and better ways?
- What pipelines will you use to best serve these customers?
- What is your overriding promise to all your customers (old and new)?
- What gross margins do you expect to generate? (What is the breakeven revenue level in your foundation building plan? What is your first revenue target level in your thrive plan?)
- How are you going to expand your "value gap" as you thrive? (Task a team to continuously lower costs and increase gross margins.)

- Who do you need on board to best serve this target customer group?

You should have all of this knowledge and information integrated into the plans that you can share with your management and staff. The more they understand how you expect to move toward surviving and growing the business, the more they can help. They have a vested interest in seeing your business survive and thrive just as much as you do. Make sure they not only understand the strategies you have adopted, but why they are important in a transforming marketplace. (You should put systems in place to help them apply the driving strategies and tactics every day.)

SWOT (Strengths, Weaknesses, Opportunities, Threats) and Ratio Analysis are good planning and assessment tools. As the industry changes, you want to get updated industry information to add to your overall knowledge base. When the time permits, go back and review the low-cost, no-cost ways to gain true market intelligence. This is the type of action that will keep you ahead of the pack to better serve your customers.

The trend reporting outline in Appendix A will help you put a reporting system in place to provide feedback so you can adjust your plans and actions as needed. Early in the survival phase, you want to be on top of all such developments daily and personally. Once you move into the foundation planning time period, you can begin to rely more on this reporting structure. It is good to remember that all the primary drivers of your business should be trended for analysis.

As you step further into the thrive planning period, you may need to acquire capital equipment to improve the cost equation or the delivery metrics. The information in Appendix B outlines a process to achieve superior results with such investment decisions. As you move down this road, it is going to be particularly important not to place excessive debt service requirements on the company. Do not get so far away from the crisis you are in that you forget some of the difficult lessons learned.

Keep an eye out for government actions. They may have helped you survive. But they may implement new regulations that will directly impact your plans. Keep as up-to-date as you can be in these areas to minimize these risks.

The other risk that can creep up on you is a lack of diversification. Once you are into the foundation building phase, make an effort to find balanced customer growth. Ideally, you do not want any single customer to account for more than 15 percent of your revenues as the business matures.

Similarly, if you have a critical vendor, see if you can find a second source to reduce that risk of a "someday" disruption. And, finally, look at your sales and marketing team as it is developing. You want to build a balance into that area so that no single person is responsible for more than 25 percent of total revenue. None of this will be easy. It is however of maximum importance to keep you from finding yourself in a new period of business distress caused by one of these sources of risk.

Businesses run on percentages (Revenue growth, gross margins, net profit)! As you progress, compare your results with the industry percentages. Keep your business on track to be in the top tier of your industry. Measuring and planning for these continuous improvements is the final step in the thrive planning and action process. Revisit the discussion on holding or expanding gross margins if you need another shot of that mental medicine.

Improving business performance, measured as net cash flow, is your ultimate financial reward for developing the right plans and executing them properly. Use these funds to build a cash reserve. Once that is accomplished, try to find a creative and balanced way to have all the employees who made the difference share in this reward.

Your three plans should each be summarized on to a single sheet of paper. This is what the management professionals refer to as a "One Page Business Plan." (It is not really a plan ... it is a summary for your daily use.) There are a number of good books on using this planning approach. Exhibit 1 offers you a template to use. The power for you is in your daily reference to these three summary documents and the "One Page Project" outline (there is a project template in Exhibit 2.). You should look at them each day as you work through the distinct phases of your three plans.

The plan summaries mirror the planning process steps in that they show the results from applying research knowledge and analysis. The key elements are these:

- Clear goals and objectives for each planning phase
- Strategies to be applied to reach the objectives
- Projects (no more than three to five per phase) to move toward the objectives
- Feedback mechanism to measure progress and to adjust the plans as indicated

These are your plans. If necessary, fix them. Change them. Make them work for you and your customers. You developed them in a truly short time due to the distressed situation that prompted this review cycle. Details within a set of plans are not always perfect. The work to find and outline the right strategies is much more critical.

The project summaries will remind you as you start each day ... exactly:

- what you and your team are to be doing
- how you are to be doing it
- when actions are to be done

- who is responsible for each action
- why you designed these project steps in this sequence

It is all too easy to get burdened by new problems each day. By using this simple set of summaries and consulting them daily, you should be able to maintain the needed focus to survive, shape a new foundation, and then thrive. This happens when you structure your survival so you can construct a durable business plan to thrive that is:

- Customer-oriented
- Quality-oriented
- Performance-oriented
- Action-oriented
- Long-term-oriented

In good times and bad, excellent business owners and their managers find ways to create productive organizations based on sound business strategies. Keep your sights on higher heights. You may be amazed at how quickly you will be on your way to reaching those goals. Do not forget Chuck Noll's words of wisdom. Congratulate yourself for starting the journey.

CHAPTER 23

LEAD THE WAY ... IT IS UP TO YOU

One person, one decision, one action can make a monumental difference more times than not. You are the one person who can help your business survive. There may be other individuals who can help you. That is great! But that is a bonus. Know that there may be more than one action that will separate you from achieving average and superior results. Take a look at history and remind yourself that you can make a huge difference.

A lot has been written over the years about the "Power of One"! Here is a recap of several events that are often references to make this important point. The margin of one vote cast by Senator Edward A. Hannegan of Indiana made Texas a part of the United States in 1845. As a matter of fact, California, Oregon, and Washington were also admitted to statehood by margins of one vote. And the draft act of World War II passed the House of Representatives in Washington by one vote.

Thomas Jefferson and John Quincy Adams were each elected president by one vote in the Electoral College. Rutherford B. Hayes' election as president was contested and referred to an electoral commission. This commission confirmed his election by one vote. That vote was cast by a congressman from Indiana who had won *his* election by one vote. This congressman was a lawyer, and the one vote that elected him was cast by a client of his who was ill but insisted on being taken to the polls to vote for him.

Never underestimate the power of ONE.

Do not get bewildered about the complexity or magnitude of a distressing environment and the related business problems. Everything breaks down into a series of *ones*. Take one step forward, and you are on your way.

It is always the next ONE that counts.

Pass this along to your management team to get that extra thought and effort that can make the critical difference in the performance of YOUR business. Survive and thrive with one thoughtful action at a time. Take full advantages of all the opportunities you have at hand. Do not get off track. Keep taking one step at a time to work through the crisis you are in. With some effort you can get to a point where your positive attitude and business momentum will begin to carry you forward.

You are the ONE and only ONE who can drive the plans for twelve to fifteen months of change for your business now. Do it "quickly" without hurrying! Take two weeks (twelve thinking and working days) to develop the plans. Monitor and measure as you implement the plans. Change them by gathering solid market information. Keep a focus on your Thrive Strategies and the related benefits of success. These are the benefits for you and your broader "business family"!

SURVIVE and THRIVE

in a BUSINESS CRISIS

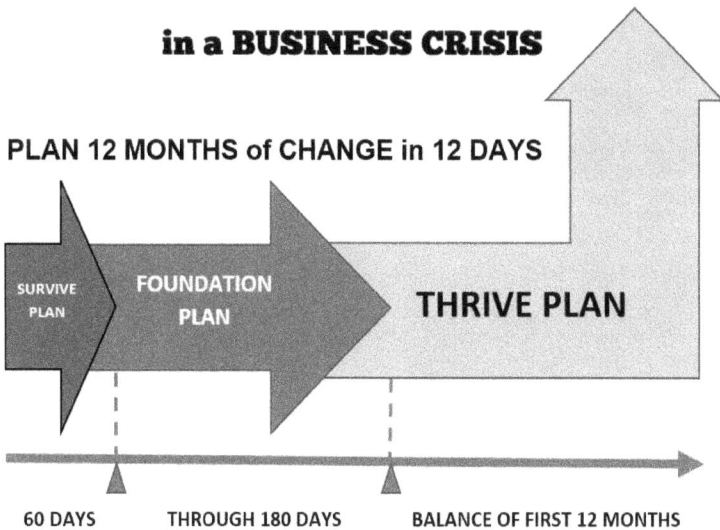

PLAN 12 MONTHS of CHANGE in 12 DAYS

SURVIVE PLAN

FOUNDATION PLAN

THRIVE PLAN

| 60 DAYS | THROUGH 180 DAYS | BALANCE OF FIRST 12 MONTHS |

A thought to remember! Create your future one action at a time!

APPENDIXES

Give yourself
more
control
of your financial future

TREND REPORTING

A Powerful Underutilized Management Tool

Effective Reporting Systems (ERSs) should provide for accountability and trend analysis. A tracking system for programs, projects, and tasks should help focus management on the detailed steps that are necessary to complete each project. This is especially true when more than the normal amount of change is upon you. The task is to match the reporting to the need. You always want to have the information required to make the best decisions you can. So, early in your survive-then-thrive process, take a few extra moments to determine what it is that you must know and when to manage your way forward.

A weekly trend analysis information system should cover most of the important operating data. Management at all levels is going to have to carefully control costs and promote growth. *This type of reporting tool will help spot trends early.* This type of system is also an effective way to have selected members of the management team become aware of the operating characteristics of the business and to **highlight areas of accountability**.

Some information is already tracked on weekly and monthly periods in most organizations. Four-week reporting periods are often easier to use for comparisons. This is different than the standard monthly cycle, but it offers some significant advantages. A trend analysis system is effective for various, consistent reporting periods ... weekly, monthly, quarterly, annually. This structure permits quick analysis of current periods and also comparable periods. This information can be easily picked up from daily records. Trending will give you an ability to quickly see the progression that is taking place. By using the first working day of each week, everything that is trended can be put on a comparable basis.

As enough weeks are accumulated, the historical information should be trended on a four-week (or monthly) basis. When you compare four-week periods to comparable periods, a better picture develops.

Anything of importance should be trended!

Trending permits quick analysis of sales performance in dollars of sales, numbers of calls made, numbers of prospects moved up in cycle, and more. When information is trended for critical sales factors, and/or by salesperson, customer type, and market segment, it is very useful for a sales manager.

There is no right or wrong final format as long as the elements and reporting have sufficient integrity and comparability. Each manager should develop her or his own short list of items to trend, and then work with the departmental staff to develop simple weekly reports that will focus on the critical items that relate to accountabilities and objectives.

By a quick comparison on a year-to-year basis or a period-to-period basis, **progress or problems can be immediately identified**. Every report should have the minimum information necessary to assess the target situation. If the period information is on track, the objectives will be reached as planned.

(If the four-week periods are used, after everyone becomes familiar with the report format, the weeks of the thirteen periods of the first year can be numbered. This is helpful when making year-to-year comparisons.)

One of the major benefits for management is that focusing on trend data indicates areas where changes are required. It should be recognized that the true corporate benefit will not be realized unless adjustments to plans, decisions, and actions follow to correct any negative trends, and to take advantage of opportunities.

Management should recognize that most companies are a long way from developing effective reporting. The struggle to fix this is well worth the difficulty if it provides the foundation for solid future growth. The key to growth is sales management, systems development, and a complete customer orientation at all levels. Even though the company's products and services may be infinitely superior, the customer and the company will not benefit without constant dedication to sales development and productivity improvements. Use of an effective reporting system will help management identify the required actions to ensure that this progress occurs.

CAPITAL BUDGETING

A Recurring Management Opportunity

Performance enhancement is the result of doing many, many things right.

Effective budgeting to provide for capital requirements and to control operating costs are critical parts of the effort to increase business value over time. As you are exerting the efforts to conserve cash and find the right adjustments to your business operating model, investment of needed capital is low on the list. In such an environment, you want to focus on using capital prudently to accelerate required operating changes. Each potential investment must past that test as well as address those in this process outline.

The process of developing operating and capital budgets should be viewed as an opportunity to test and adjust strategies and tactics. Ultimately, the management of any enterprise is about effectiveness and efficiency. Budgeting is a process that should address both effectiveness and efficiency. The capital budgeting process will always have three elements that ultimately affect operating results.

All expenditures of capital fall into three capital budget groups. They are

1. Revenue enhancement
2. Maintenance of present capacity
3. Change to the operating process

Operating budget considerations must then analyze the strategies chosen in the capital budgeting process and strive to constantly increase efficiency. When the limits are reached in efficiency development, a change in the way the work is done must be considered. That point of departure then drives or prompts future capital budget considerations.

Effectiveness **is doing the right things.**
While *Efficiency* **is doing things right.**

Operating and capital budgeting require the determination of what are the right things to do *(Effectiveness)* and how to do what is planned in the right way. *(Efficiency.)* To accomplish these dual management goals requires integrated planning of all budgets. The business planning and budgeting process and procedures should provide this opportunity to review the chosen business strategies and the departmental operating tactics.

Economic depreciation versus accounting depreciation is an important concept to grasp. For each capital or operation expenditure, there are two critical management determinations: The first is the "driver" and "function" of the item or expenditure. *(Revenue enhancement, maintenance of capacity, change in the operation process.)* The second is the economic life of the new asset. Obviously, any item with an economic life of one year or less should be expensed, while items with an anticipated economic life of greater than one year should be capitalized to properly account for multi-year benefits. Accounting and reporting standards will control the "depreciable life for accounting purposes." *(There is some flexibility accorded these "accounting determinations.")* Management should not rely directly on the "accounting life" of assets for planning purposes. **The "useful" or "economic life" of the asset must be the planning driver.**

In addition, the "function" should be a major determinate of whether an expenditure should be considered a repair and/or maintenance expense or a capital expenditure. If the expenditure specifically is required only to maintain the operating integrity of an item and not to extend the life of the item, it may be correctly considered a repair expense. However, within either definition of "asset life," consistency of the estimate of either "economic" or "account" life of an asset is important. Such an approach should result initially in a plan to create an annual expected replacement expenditure. The date of original acquisition should be used to prompt planning, but the review process should not rely solely on the age of equipment to develop plans.

Return on Investment

Historically, capital budgeting in most closely held businesses has not been fully disciplined by analysis of the return on investment (ROI). In some environments, it may seem difficult to apply standard investment measurement methods. Although ROI analysis may be difficult conceptually to use in replacement analysis, this is not the case with major projects. **All projects that drive strategic operating changes must be thoroughly analyzed. Such projects should not be approved unless they will provide a return equal to the cost of capital plus a risk factor that reflects any uncertainty in the anticipated revenue stream and operating costs.**

A comparative analysis on all replacement planning should be instituted. The mathematics associated with this analysis should be carefully understood. Analysis often does not have to provide for consideration of mid-year present value applications or other refinements to enhance the process. An alternative method would be to employ the simpler "payback period method" for all investments below a threshold investment amount. Initially, an investment threshold can be adapted and rechecked over time to assess the benefits of detailed analysis. Replacement, maintenance, repairs, and actions to simply maintain facilities or other assets required to continue operations will always appear difficult to analyze. **However, in all investment decisions, there are alternatives or substitutions.** The necessity for management to consider and study an alternative approach or substitute products should be driven by an "investment" approach to capital budgeting. In many cases, alternatives or substitutes may not be readily evident. **It is the thinking process employed to discover optional ways to reach the same objective that will help optimize investment decisions.** It could be a situation as simple as finding out that a new piece of equipment with cost-saving features will be available in six or twelve months. Thus, a delay in the purchase decision may provide cumulative advantages. A consistent management orientation that causes all "investments" to be reviewed and tested and retested will often deliver notably superior value and desired benefits.

The general questions are these:

1. Is this the best way to solve this problem?
2. What alternatives were considered?
3. Are there any benefits or impacts from delaying this decision?

Operating and Capital Budgets Should Crossover

Budget planning, monitoring, and controlling for all Income Statement expenses is critical to overall management activity. The planning process provides an opportunity to reconsider capital investments to reduce operational expenses. The development of trend information is critical to prompt activities of this nature. A review of the income statement for the business will show the relative size and importance of wages, salaries, benefits, and taxes. Often these items comprise a significant percentage of total operating costs.

Staff planning for the anticipated operating levels should include **an interactive analysis to prompt management thinking about "How the work is done" as well as ways to comply with key system needs and drivers**. If wage and related expenses were to increase faster than the increase in unit revenue over a period of years, structural staffing changes may be required. This focus on effectiveness and the resulting situation analysis may indicate a need for a greater level of capital spending. Managers will need to interactively assess long-term capital costs and annual operating costs. The business owner must be in a position to study, plan, and fund required operational changes to meet critical challenges. The repairs and maintenance budget are the complement to the capital budget. (Repairing or upgrading of tired assets to reduce maintenance costs and to increase efficiency can be a useful approach that should not be overlooked.) Increased repairs may slow or reduce capital expenditures. The classification of these expenses is always a point for discussion. *(Although all operating*

budgets can be improved by adopting a dynamic bud-
geting approach, this is less important for the repair and
maintenance budget.)

Multi-Year Planning Model

Typically, a multi-year cash flow planning model should
be developed to permit iteration with various scenarios.
(Your thrive plans should include capital deployment
within the principles outlined. In that regard, leasing
options to preserve cash initially may be an important
consideration.) The model should be simple to integrate by making changes in major activity-driven budget
assumptions and should take fully into account all system constraints. **Such a model should be used to provide an early indication that strategic or operational
changes should be considered.** Both capital budgeting
and operational budgeting plans should be developed
only after a full assessment of the existing business
strategies and assumptions.

The use and continuous improvement of such a
model is especially important in an environment that
has a high degree of change and/or increasing competition. Strategic changes and optimizing capital budgets
should provide the business owner with the opportunity
to maintain the company's competitive advantages and
resulting performance. It is important to make assessments and to make changes early. **If funds are spent
on operations in a sub-par structure, those funds are**

gone and cannot be applied to an investment that can optimize the operating environment. Both the capital budgeting and operating budgeting process can be used to create an environment with lower risks.

Summary

Capital budgeting is not a stand-alone process. To effectively make investment decisions, capital budgeting must be integrated with operational budgeting and testing of strategic plans and operating tactics. In this way, the capital budget can be optimized and can drive the annual planning process. The opportunity is available for management to make changes to enhance organizational performance. To accomplish this, a multi-year interactive planning model, the effective grouping of capital assets for review and control, and effective grouping of operating accounts to improve monthly budget reports should be the minimum tools employed by a business owner.

Disciplined use of "Payback" or "Return on Investment" analysis should assure optimization of the operational impact of all investments. Dynamic *(flexible)* budgeting can be implemented, when indicated, to improve the utility of management reports. In addition, trend analysis, which provides for period-to-period comparisons, should be developed and used to provide additional impetus for timely decision-making and planning.

HOW TO CREATE VALUE WITH ACQUISITIONS

By most measures, the majority of acquisitions do not realize their financial objectives. To improve these results, a clear focus on the objectives and value creation is a must. **There have been many studies of mergers and acquisitions that unfortunately offer limited insight into**

What to do! *and* Why to do it!

The fuzzy information in most of the analysis and review in this area is the result of poorly stated strategies or hidden strategies in merger and acquisition planning. Far too many transactions have cost reduction as the primary driver ... even though the explicitly stated objectives are quite different. In addition, "industry roll-ups" and "purchases of depressed assets" rarely yield the promised returns-on-investment.

A better approach is to follow the logic spelled out by Goedhart, Koller and Wessels in a 2010 article in

Corporate Finance Practice. These professionals outlined a simple reference list for use in developing and executing acquisition strategies that can and should increase business value. Specifically, they (G, K & W) argue that **to create value, a planned acquisition should be solidly based one or more of the following strategies**:

Improving the performance of the target company. *(This objective must be based on existing knowledge and management expertise.)*

Removing excess capacity from an industry. *(In the middle-market, this strategy is only operative in smaller market segments.)*

Acquiring skills, products, or technology faster or at a lower cost versus internal development. *(These new assets must be applied to a known market.)*

Creating market access for products. *(Finding new channels and customer base for existing products as part of established growth processes.)*

Identifying early-stage developing companies that have a competitive edge. *(This approach requires a willingness to invest in growth.)*

Each transaction must have its own strategic logic. This is especially true in a disrupted economy when the future is less certain! Successful acquirers have the discipline to insist on a well-defined objective and an easily understood acquisition plan before moving ahead with any potential deal. In many cases, these experienced managers have an overall corporate development strategy based on a deep understanding of the risks and rewards of moving in the matrix, as presented in the following graphic.

Strategic <u>Focus</u> of Efforts *(Maximize ROE)*

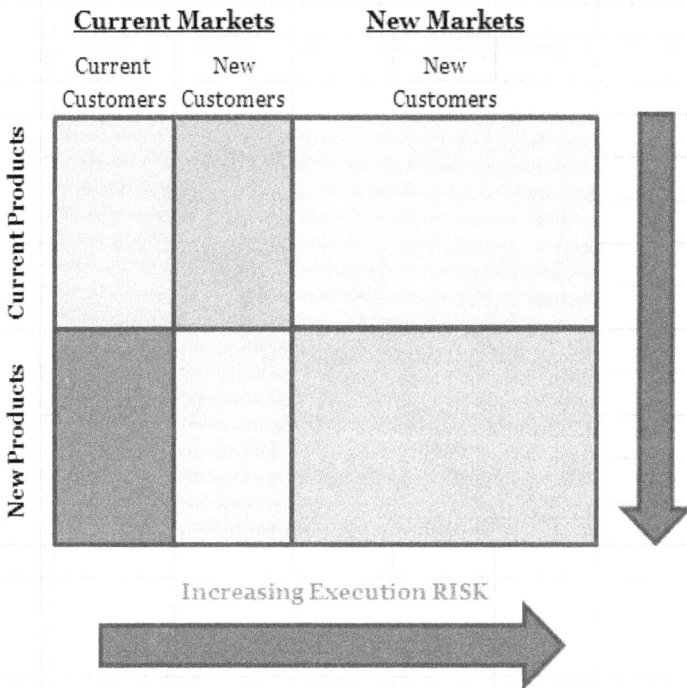

The reason the best-of-the-best acquirers succeed is that they really do not see acquisitions as a growth strategy ... but rather as a tactic to achieve planned growth within the business, product, market development matrix. These experienced business managers operate as strategists who have already applied the following recipe for success to their business planning and strategic development:

- Protect existing business with operational excellence
- Penetrate further into existing markets segments with current customers
- Extend into existing market segments with existing products
- Extend into new market segments with existing products
- Extend into existing market segments with new products
- Diversify with new products in new market segments

This approach provides these owners with the solid thinking and appropriate measure of momentum needed to execute on well-developed strategic acquisitions to further long-term business goals and objectives. For example, an acquisition could provide a new product group to offer to existing customers as a value-creating acquisition strategy.

The key is that the impetus would be from planning and assessment that an acquisition (a tactical step) was the best option available. Every business owner should make an effort to replicate this merger-and-acquisition process to **"increase business value"** with **minimal risk** and **maximum opportunity for achieving sound objectives**.

EXHIBITS

Use these templates to help develop and
use your plans on a daily basis.

Exhibit 1: One Page Plan

Focused Actions

VISION:

MISSION:

OBJECTIVES:
1
2
3
4
5
6
7

STRATEGIES:
1
2
3
4
5

PLANS/PROJECTS:
1
2
3
4
5
6
7

JUSTIFICATION/RESULTS:
1
2
3

Exhibit 2: Project Template

PROGRAM SUMMARY

OBJECTIVE(S):

ACTION PROGRAM:

ASSUMPTIONS:

POTENTIALS:

STRATEGY:

PROJECTS TACTICS: (ACTION STEPS IN SEQUENCE)   SCHEDULE   Mgr. Responsible

1
2
3
4
5
6

RESOURCES REQUIRED: (ASSETS, COSTS, TIME, SPACE, ETC.)

1   MONEY:
2   PERSONNEL:
3   MATERIALS:
4   OTHER:

COST/BENEFIT: PURPOSE/RESULTS: (Why do it?)

1   COST:
2   BENEFIT:

ALTERNATIVES CONSIDERED:

FINAL INFORMATION

With consistent thought and effort you can step from the long tunnel into the sunlight.

ACKNOWLEDGEMENTS

In almost every book, the author thanks individuals who were most instrumental in helping him or her develop and complete the book. There are a few folks who must be thanked due to their direct or indirect contributions. This book is no different in that regard.

I would like to thank a young English major who motivated me to learn to write a long time ago, and two early mentors who taught me that the best way to address bureaucratic friction is to focus on the underlying truth and facts. I am constantly assisted from hearing many great management consultants and investment banking advisors in my ear. They taught me and many others how to get things done in the right way for the right reasons. This book, which in this manner is similar to both my international best-selling book, **When Is the Right Time to Sell My Business?,** and the follow-up book titled **How Can I Increase the Value of My Business?** reflects that fundamental action-oriented approach.

My editor, whom I could not write without, knows more about written communications than most English professors. She has made the difference in getting this book into your hands. I want to thank her for doing the best she could with an engineer-turned-author to improve this book for your benefit.

There are many, many other people to thank who have helped me over my varied career. This list varies from the sponsors of the many valuation seminars I have been privileged to present, to the founders of the Institute of Business Appraisers and other professional organizations. What is offered for consideration in this book was learned from these valuation and transaction advisors as well as from many clients who successfully worked through challenging times.

OTHER RESOURCES

MergerMentor.com is "the" educational website designed for business owners interested in professionally improving the value of their businesses. It provides valuation information, transaction articles, checklists, and planning templates for use in the process. This is also the place to add knowledge on how to sell your business quickly and quietly at the right time for the right price.

Registration is now FREE for Business Owners! Please take this opportunity to learn all you can about how to reduce business risks and to improve performance. Merger Mentor gives you relevant and actionable information to help you manage important changes in your business.

**To become a member of Merger Mentor,
go to the link below:
www.MergerMentor.com
(FREE Access for Business Owners)**

ABOUT THE AUTHOR

Richard Mowrey is an expert in the valuation and sale of privately held businesses with a reputation for getting the job done quickly and quietly, at the right price. He has shown countless business owners how early access to comprehensive, easy-to-use information can be effectively applied to dramatically increase the value of their businesses.

Richard's first book, **When Is the Right Time to Sell My Business?** was recognized as a #1 international best seller. One of the three expert answers to that title question (provided in depth in that first book) is "When the business is ready." Richard's second book, **How to Increase the Value of My Business?** endeavored to provide the reader with some additional tools and techniques to help improve business performance.

Richard has owned and operated four businesses and bases his books on the knowledge he acquired from over forty years spent as both a business owner and a hands-on ownership transition advisor. He has been an active member of the board of directors of many businesses and has a wealth of knowledge and practical experience.

Richard is a sought-after speaker on valuation and ownership transfer topics. He has presented educational courses in valuation and transactional planning, and has taught at Wentworth Institute of Technology, Rollins College, and Indiana University of Pennsylvania, as well as for the International Business Brokers Association (IBBA), and the M&A Source, which is the largest international organization of business intermediaries.

Richard is a Fellow of the IBBA and has held, during his long career, the following certifications: Certified Management Accountant (CMA) from the Institute of Certified Management Accountants, Certified Business Appraiser (CBA) from the Institute of Business Appraisers, and Certified Business Intermediary (CBI) from the International Business Brokers Association, as well as other certifications and designations. He holds a BS in Mechanical Engineering and an MS in Management Science from Rensselaer Polytechnic Institute.

HOW TO CONTACT THE AUTHOR

For information on virtual workshops or other seminar planning materials, please visit www.RichMowrey.com. For further information or to contact the author regarding a speaking engagement, please visit or call Richard Mowrey directly at **(814) 938-8170.**

A REQUEST

I wrote this book to help business owners acquire the ability to gain a lot of useful, actionable knowledge in a short period. This critically important information was learned from a variety of professional advisors and educators over many years. It has proven, when effectively applied, to help dramatically improve business performance. I trust it has done that for you. If so, would you **please leave a review on Amazon** to help other business owners gain from the important content in this book?